NATIONAL GEOGRAPHIC KIDS

Brain Bogglers

Stephanie Warren Drimmer
with puzzles by
Julie K. Cohen

Over **100** GAMES and PUZZLES to Unravel the Mysteries of Your Mind

NATIONAL GEOGRAPHIC

WASHINGTON, D.C.

Contents

CHAPTER ONE

Back for More?

IMA GENIUS
CERTIFIED MASTERMIND

Greetings, Mastermind.

Ima Genius here, your host for this book and fellow Mastermind. When last we met, I helped you grow from puny pea brain to full-on cranial champion. Now your brain bulges so big it could probably bench-press your body! Ha! I kid. Only my mind is that mighty.

After all that hard work, you refused my once-in-a-lifetime offer to join E.V.I.L.—the Extraordinarily Villainous Intelligence League. Instead, you signed on with those lame-o goody-goodies at G.O.O.D.—the Geniuses of Outstanding Decency. What were you thinking?

Well, that was a mistake, Mastermind.

Once, we could have been allies, uniting our E.V.I.L. genius to take over the world. But now we are enemy eggheads and rivals of reasoning. It's time to duke it out in a cranium-to-cranium challenge!

In this book, we'll test our superior skulls with science stories so strange they'd make Einstein admit defeat. Then we'll face off with games and puzzles that could stump even the most exceptional egghead.

Think you're up for the challenge? Ha—good luck! I hope you brought your grade-A game face, Mastermind, because this is going to be an all-out superbrain showdown!

Ima Genius

P.S. Oh yes, and let's not forget about my smarty sidekick, Atom. He may be a dog, but don't be fooled—he's more intelligent than most people. Just don't rub his belly, OK? He might follow you right out of my lab.

ATOM
CANINE CRANIAL CHAMPION

Making the Most of Mastermind

YOU DIDN'T GET THIS BOOK JUST FOR MY WITTY WISECRACKS. A superpowered skull like yours is here to learn. Let these eggheaded extras take your brainbuilding to the next level.

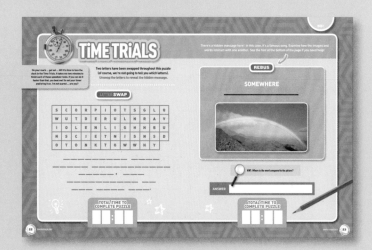

Time Trials

On your mark, get set ... GO! Think fast for these timed tests in each chapter. To beat me, you're going to need to complete these puzzles in less than two minutes. Write down your times so you can gloat at how they improve as your noggin grows stronger. Lesser eggheads, take note!

Tips and Tricks

Keep your eyes open for Atom and me to show up on the page. Listen to what we say—we often have hints to help jog your noggin. Other times, we want to play fetch ... OK, that's just Atom.

Ima Genius's Brainiac Bonus

So you think you're pretty clever, huh? Put that Mastermind to the test with these brain busters, the trickiest puzzles I could think of. Get them right and you'll be a true brainiac.

Atom's Brain Break

Even big brains get tired sometimes. Atom entertains your noggin with these silly-but-true facts. What a canine clown!

Myths Busted!

Most people think the myths on these pages are true ... but you're too smart for that! Learn the true story and impress your friends and family.

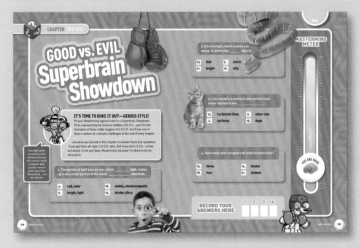

Mastermind Meter

Want to gauge how your thinker compares with mine? Keep an eye on the Mastermind Meter. Can your cranium outcompete mine to get all the way to the top?

Try your best to do all the puzzles in this book without help. But even geniuses get stuck sometimes. If that happens to you, check the back of the book to see the answers. Just use the Mastermind code of honor and don't check unless you truly need a brain boost.

What Kind of Genius Are You?

DIFFERENT BRAINS ARE GOOD AT SOLVING DIFFERENT PROBLEMS. To figure out what type of cranial cleverness you have in your skull, solve these four puzzles. Then choose the one that felt easiest to you and read the description underneath to reveal your brand of brain.

PUZZLE A

What animals or objects can you construct with these pieces by flipping, rotating, or moving them around? They do not need to stay in this order, or even be lined up.

PUZZLE B

What color should the last two objects be?

Purple   Yellow

PUZZLE C

Can you figure out how to fit the yellow, red, blue, and green sections of brick together to match the wall of black bricks (without rotating or flipping any images)?

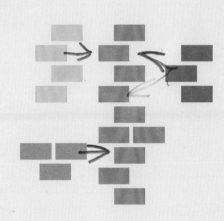

PUZZLE D

Replace one letter in each of these words.

The letter you choose must be used for all three words and must create real words.

ROT = _Cot_

BARK = _Back_

ROAST = _Coast_

PUZZLE A

CREATIVITY CHAMPION
LEONARDO DA VINCI

You're a Creativity Champion. You're great at looking at problems in a different way than other people and finding unique solutions, which may seem to come to you out of nowhere. Your creative cranium would make you a great entrepreneur—a person who dreams up business ideas and makes them real.

Leonardo Da Vinci was a painter, sculptor, architect, musician, writer, and engineer who lived from 1452 to 1519. He painted one of the most famous paintings in the world, the "Mona Lisa," and in his spare time created plans for flying machines, an armored vehicle, and solar power, just to name a few. That guy was good at everything!

LOOK FOR

GENIUS GENUS:
CREATIVITY CHAMPION

PUZZLE B

LOGICAL LEADER
MARIE CURIE

You're a Logical Leader. Your egghead is exceptionally skilled at deducing cause and effect, finding patterns, and solving problems. You can use your brainpower to figure out the answers to all kinds of questions. That could make you a talented engineer or scientist.

Marie Curie was a chemist who lived from 1867 to 1934. She is famous for experiments that helped discover radioactivity, or what happens when elements spontaneously emit energy. (It's what powers x-ray machines that can see through your skin.) She was the first person to win two Nobel Prizes for her work. Now that's some genius girl power!

LOOK FOR

GENIUS GENUS:
LOGICAL LEADER

PUZZLE C

SPATIAL SUPERSTAR
ALBERT EINSTEIN

You're a Spatial Superstar. That means your brain is talented at understanding and remembering where objects are. Your supersense helps you read maps, solve mazes, and visualize how objects interact in space. Your spatial skull would make you a good explorer, Web designer, or architect.

Albert Einstein was a physicist who lived from 1879 to 1955. He is most famous for devising the theory of general relativity, which explains how planets in outer space orbit around one another. Einstein was known for being able to create complex mathematical theories just by visualizing how objects move in space!

LOOK FOR → **GENIUS GENUS:** SPATIAL SUPERSTAR

PUZZLE D

WORD WIZARD
WILLIAM SHAKESPEARE

You're a Word Wizard. You have a knack for reading and language, and you're great at puzzles involving words. With your wordy wisdom, you might grow up to be a writer or an editor—or even a crossword puzzle creator.

William Shakespeare was a writer who lived from 1564 to 1616. He was such a witty wordsmith that the English language sometimes wasn't enough for him: When he needed a turn of phrase that it didn't have, he would invent one. Without Shakespeare, we wouldn't say things like "wild goose chase," "dead as a doornail," or even "knock knock—who's there?"

LOOK FOR → **GENIUS GENUS:** WORD WIZARD

Brain Basics

ARE YOU SCRATCHING YOUR HEAD, wondering what makes your thinker tick? I thought so. Get familiar with your brain with this genius guide.

Occipital lobe

MENTAL MAP

Skull: Like a helmet, protects your brain from injury

Brain stem: Connects the brain to the body and controls basic functions like heartbeat and breathing

Thalamus: Sends sensory information—what you see, hear, touch, taste, and smell—to your cerebrum for analysis

Hypothalamus: Regulates hunger, sleep, and body temperature

Cerebellum: Helps control movement

Cerebrum: The biggest part of the brain, it's in charge of all our conscious actions and thoughts. It also analyzes sensory information and stores memories. The cerebellum is made up of lobes that handle different tasks:

Occipital lobe: Processes information from the eyes

Parietal lobe: Processes sensory information such as taste, temperature, and touch

Temporal lobe: Processes sound

Frontal lobe: Responsible for higher mental processes like thinking, making decisions, speaking, and emotions

FUNFACT

An ancient Greek named Galen was one of the first people to have a hunch that the brain was an important organ. What gave him this brainy idea? He was a surgeon who treated the gory head wounds of gladiators!

NERVE NETWORK

Your brain is connected to a network of nerve cells, or **neurons.** Think of the nervous system like a tree with branches that sprout from your spinal cord and extend to every corner of your body.

Your brain and your body use this nerve network to communicate with each other. For example, when you pick up something cold, like an ice cube, a signal called a **nerve impulse** travels from your hand up to your brain. Your brain processes the signal, decides, "That's cold!" and sends a signal back down to your hand telling you to put down the ice.

That might sound like a long process, but nerve impulses travel fast—at 150 miles an hour (241 km/h)!

So what powers this marvelous mental machine? I'll give you a hint: You might find the answer *shocking!* Stumped? It's electricity! Nerve impulses are electrical signals that travel along neurons, which conduct electricity like wires.

Parietal lobe

Frontal lobe

Temporal lobe

Cerebellum

Brain stem

DOUBLE-SIDED

Each side, or **hemisphere,** of your brain controls one half of your body. But here's the twisted part: The right hemisphere controls the left side of your body, and the left hemisphere controls the right side of your body. So if you want to move your right hand, the command comes from the left side of your brain. Weird, huh?

Each hemisphere has special talents, but the two sides have to work together. In most people, the left hemisphere is in control of language. But the right hemisphere handles mental images. That means that if you're reading a book and creating picture of what's happening in your mind, you're using both sides at once. What teamwork!

Mysteries of the Mind

RIDDLE ME THIS, MASTERMIND: WHAT'S THE BIGGEST MYSTERY IN SCIENCE? Don't be silly—it's not how the Earth formed or what killed the dinosaurs. Many scientists say that the most puzzling puzzle of all is sitting right between your ears. That's right—it's your brain.

Experts have been getting brain basics all wrong since the ancient Egyptians reached into mummies' nostrils to pull their brains out of their heads (yes, really!) around 3000 B.C. Certain the heart was where thoughts came from, the Egyptians carefully preserved that organ and threw the brain out with the trash. Whoopsie. Scientists have gotten a little smarter since then—but they still have more questions than answers about what makes a thinker tick.

Since you've got a critical cranium on top of your shoulders, you might be asking: What's so tricky about the brain? It weighs only three pounds (1.4 kg), for goodness' sake. It's not very intimidating. Are brain scientists just sad slackers?

Those are good questions, Mastermind. But consider this: The brain might be small, but it's incredibly complex. There are as many nerve cells, or **neurons,** in the brain as there are stars in the Milky Way—about 100 billion. All of these neurons

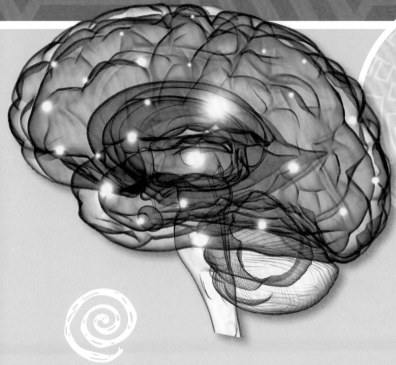

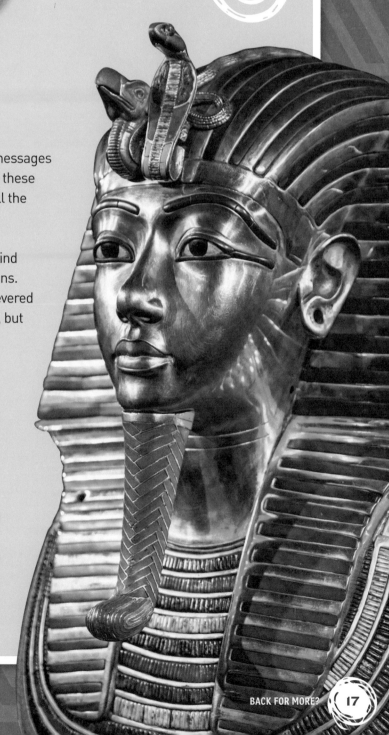

FUNFACT
The brain uses 20 percent of the body's energy.

are connected to each other, shooting electricity-powered messages back and forth every moment of your life. There are more of these connections in your head than there are grains of sand on all the beaches of Earth—about 100 *trillion!*

Getting the picture, Mastermind? Understanding how the mind works is a task that would boggle even the brawniest of brains. Modern science means we're able to reattach someone's severed hand or swap out a malfunctioning heart for a better model, but figuring out the human brain is a much bigger challenge.

It's a tough task, but brain scientists have pushed forward anyway. And today, they have technologies like **Magnetic Resonance Imaging (MRI)** machines—which scan the brain using magnets—to peer inside skulls in brand-new ways. The things they've discovered are starting to unravel the mysteries of the mind.

In this book, you'll discover some of the things they've found out. It's time to learn some of the secrets of the stranger inside your own skull: your brain. But be warned, Mastermind, what you learn about your own noggin might surprise you.

CHAPTER TWO

Open Your Eyes ?

Look around. What you see in front of you is what's really there ... right? Ha! Not so fast, Mastermind. Consider this: The images your eyes capture aren't very impressive. They're just a pair of tiny, two-dimensional, upside-down pictures.

So how come you see one single, large, three-dimensional, right-side-up, very detailed world? That's where your brain comes in. Your noggin does a lot of fancy guesswork to flip the images, make them bigger, and fill in essential information like motion, shape, texture, brightness, distance, and depth.

If you think about it, your brain does a lot more seeing than your eyes do. And, as you're about to find out, what your brain decides to show you isn't always what's truly there.

Don't believe me? Read on!

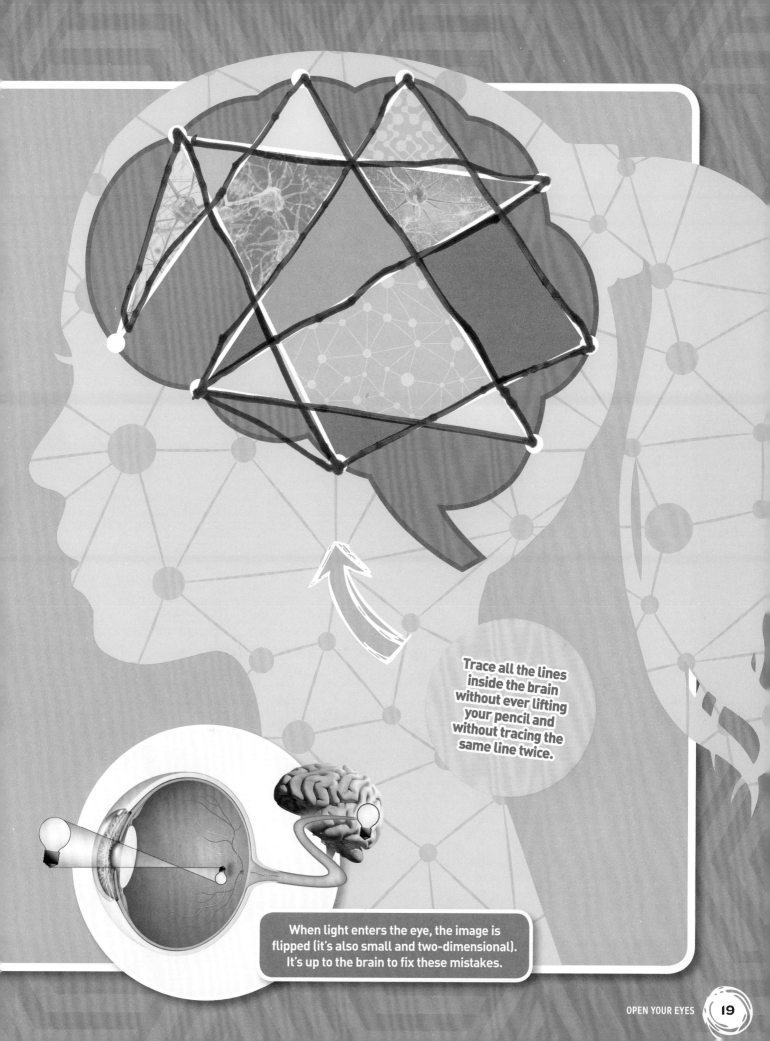

Trace all the lines inside the brain without ever lifting your pencil and without tracing the same line twice.

When light enters the eye, the image is flipped (it's also small and two-dimensional). It's up to the brain to fix these mistakes.

See What You're Missing

AS YOU READ THIS SENTENCE, you are being bombarded by waves of **electromagnetic energy.** These waves are carrying TV shows, radio pop songs, cell phone conversations, x-rays, and much more. But you don't notice most of them—they go right through your body!

These electromagnetic energy waves come in a spectrum of sizes, from small to big. Your eyes have special sensors that detect a section of medium-size waves. These waves—called **visible light**—are how you see everything around you.

But visible light makes up less than one ten-trillionth of all the electromagnetic energy that's out there. That's a very teensy-tiny section! The rest is invisible to human eyes.

If your eyes had a different type of sensor, the world around you would look totally different. If you had x-ray eyes, you'd see in x-ray vision! If your eyes could sense gamma rays, you'd see rays beaming in from exploding stars in space.

Some lucky animals can do this. They sense energy waves that are invisible to you. No fair, right? Check out the pictures at right to find out what your human eyes are missing out on.

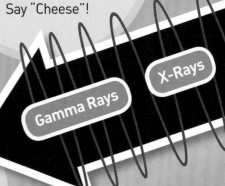

X-Rays
Hot gases in space emit these waves. Doctors also use them to see through your skin and snap a photo of your bones. Say "Cheese"!

Gamma Rays | X-Rays

Gamma Rays
Gamma rays are super-high-energy waves created by things like exploding stars, lightning, and nuclear explosions. Physicians harness their power to kill cancer cells.

Infrared Light

To your wimpy human eyes, a mouse is invisible at night. But to a rattlesnake, the mouse glows in the dark! Rattlesnakes have an extra sense organ that detects infrared light, which is emitted by warm objects. No light? No problem. It's still snack time.

Radio Waves

Radio stations beam radio waves carrying your favorite songs through the air. Your radio captures them and turns them into sound so you can hear them. Stars also emit radio waves. Scientists use giant radio antennas to capture them and learn about how stars are born.

Visible Light

This tiny sliver represents the only waves you can see. Bet you didn't know you were so shortsighted!

Radio Waves

Microwaves

Infrared Light

Visible Light

Ultraviolet Energy

Ultraviolet Energy

Butterflies may be simple insects, but they can see something that humans can't: ultraviolet light. With human vision, a butterfly may look plain, but with butterfly vision, she glows with bright patterns! Scientists think butterflies use these ultraviolet patterns to send secret messages. The colors say things—like "Come on over to my flower!"—that other butterflies can see but hungry predators can't. Cool trick!

Microwaves

Stars and other objects in space emit microwaves. You can also use them to heat up your lunch in just a few minutes. *Beep, beep!*

TIME TRIALS

On your mark ... get set ... GO! It's time to face the clock in the Time Trials. It takes me two minutes to finish each of these speedster tests. If you can do it faster than that, you beat me! So set your timer and bring it on. I'm not scared ... are you?

Two letters have been swapped throughout this puzzle (of course, we're not going to tell you *which* letters).
Unswap the letters to reveal the hidden message.

LETTER **SWAP**

S	C	O	R	P	I	O	T	S	G	L	O
W	U	T	D	E	R	U	L	N	R	A	V
I	O	L	E	N	L	I	G	H	N	B	U
N	S	C	I	E	T	N	I	S	N	S	D
O	T	O	N	K	T	O	W	W	H	Y

Scorpions Glow
under oltrviolet
light, But
scientists do
not know why.

TOTAL TIME TO COMPLETE PUZZLE

| 0 | 0 | : | D | 12 |

There's a hidden message here! In this case, it's a famous song. Examine how the images and words interact with one another. See the hint at the bottom of the page if you need help!

REBUS

SOMEWHERE

_____

HINT: Where is the word compared to the picture?

ANSWER

TOTAL TIME TO COMPLETE PUZZLE

Sight Stunts

AS A PROUD MEMBER OF THE CANINE SPECIES, I call cats my sworn enemy. Those whiskered furballs think they're something special— just because they don't drool! But even I have to admit that cats helped scientists make a big discovery when it comes to vision. Just listen to this:

VERTICAL VISION

In the 1960s, scientists decided that it was time to learn more about how vision works. So they called in the sharpest seers they knew: cats.

The scientists divided kittens into two groups. They put one group into a world made completely of vertical (top-to-bottom) lines. The walls of the kittens' enclosures were covered with black-and-white-striped wallpaper. The people feeding them even wore vertical stripes on their clothes. For the first few weeks of the cats' lives, they saw only vertical lines.

The scientists raised the other group of kittens in a world of only horizontal (left-to-right) lines. These kittens never saw vertical lines. When the cats in both groups were a few weeks old, the scientists let them out of their enclosures and into the world. What happened was

MYTHS
BUSTED!

MYTH: Bats are blind.

BUSTED!: Many bats use echolocation to get around. But all can see.

Flexible Brain

The cat vision experiment taught scientists that childhood is a very important time for brain training. When you're young, your brain is flexible and can learn all kinds of things. But once you grow up, learning new skills becomes much trickier.

Consider the infamous case of a girl known as Genie. Until she was 13 years old, Genie had almost no contact with other people. Nobody spoke to her, so she didn't learn how to talk. Even though scientists later tried to teach her, she could never really learn how to speak. Just like the cats that were blind to lines, Genie's sad story shows that if a young brain isn't exposed to something early, it might not be able to catch up later.

So go out and learn, young Mastermind! Try picking up Japanese, or learning tennis, or playing the guitar. With a bendy brain like yours, you'll be a pro in no time!

astonishing. The cats raised in the horizontal world were blind to all vertical lines: They could jump up onto a chair seat for a nap but would bump into the chair's legs. The cats raised in the vertical world were just the opposite—they could weave around the chair legs with ease but didn't know the seat was there to snooze on.

This experiment shows that the way your brain is trained when you're young can actually change how you see the world. And what you see might not always be what's right in front of you!

FUN FACT
Cats need one-sixth the amount of light as humans to see.

Are you ready for some brain-twisting puzzles, Mastermind? Put your noggin to the test and see if you can figure these out.

Cat Eyes

by: Cat E. Ness

Unscramble the words below the spaces to complete the rhyme.

Who can see better, you _____ with more cones
(ANMUSH)

To see far-off _____, including small stones,
(SLIDTEA)

Or a cat like me who has more rods for _____ vision
(THING)

To hunt my prey, with _____ precision?
(DAYLED)

While your eyes mix greens, reds, and _____,
(ELBUS)

I see very few colors, in _____ hues.
(TIMELID)

You humans see _____ during the day,
(EGRTA)

When cats _____, sleep, and play.
(GLUEON)

While we lack your _____ to see so far,
(WEPOR)

Consider this, my _____ star....
(PURSE)

As I scrunch down low, _____ through the grasses,
(VINEWAG)

Can you imagine me, a cat, wearing your _____?
(SAGLESS)

Butterfly Code

Although we cannot show you the messages butterflies display using ultraviolet light, we can show you the types of things butterflies may say to each other. Can you figure out the messages these butterflies are sharing with one another?

HINT: Each butterfly wing has two words.

COME FLY WITH ME.

THIS IS ME FLYING.

The Woman Who Sees Extra Colors

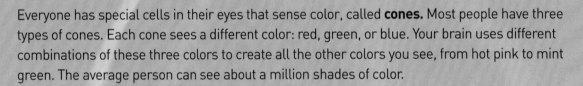

CONCETTA ANTICO IS AN ARTIST WHO PAINTS SCENES IN VIVID COLORS. In her paintings, a rock shimmers with pink. A leaf's shadow is purple. A tree is a rainbow of colors.

To create these beautiful scenes, Antico can't credit creativity alone—she actually *sees* objects this way. And when she found out that other people don't, she was shocked! Antico has a special ability—she's a **tetrochromat,** someone whose eyes have extra color-sensing cells.

Everyone has special cells in their eyes that sense color, called **cones.** Most people have three types of cones. Each cone sees a different color: red, green, or blue. Your brain uses different combinations of these three colors to create all the other colors you see, from hot pink to mint green. The average person can see about a million shades of color.

But Antico has an extra type of cone, giving her a total of four. With her extra cone, scientists think she may be able to see as many 100 million colors! It's hard for someone with three cones to imagine what extra shades Antico is seeing. But her supercolorful paintings might be a hint (see "Rainbow Eucalyptus" at left).

It gets even stranger. Turns out, tetrachromacy isn't even all that rare. Scientists estimate that about 12 percent of women have that extra cone. (Genetically, men can't be tetrachromats.) But when scientists test these tetrachromats to find out if they can see extra shades, most can't.

So what is special about Antico? Scientists aren't sure. It might be that she owes her super vision to her artist training. By paying so much attention to color, Antico might have trained her brain to process the extra colors her eyes were picking up. If all four-coned women did similar brain training, they might all start seeing colors that most of us can only imagine.

Extreme Eyes

MOST HUMANS HAVE THREE COLOR RECEPTORS IN THEIR EYES.
A few special people, like Concetta Antico, have four. Butterflies are even luckier—they have an astounding *five* color receptors.

But there is one animal that tops them all: the mantis shrimp. This visual victor has *16* color receptors!

Scientists aren't sure yet exactly how well the mantis shrimp actually sees. But it's incredible to imagine the possibilities. Think, for example, about the most spectacular sunset you've ever seen. Your brain created that view from just three colors. Now try to imagine what it would look like if your brain had 16 colors to work with: That could be what sunsets look like to a mantis shrimp. That is one special shellfish!

IMA GENIUS'S BRAINIAC BONUS: TRIANGULATION

GENIUS GENUS:
SPATIAL SUPERSTAR

For this challenge, you can use your awesome powers of imagination or you can cut out nine equal-size triangles from a piece of paper and arrange them on top of the orange triangles at right.

The challenge: Create a total of five yellow triangles by moving one orange triangle.

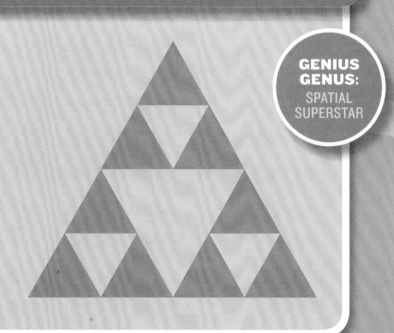

Spectrumtacular!

After you solve the crossword, unscramble the yellow squares to solve the bonus question at the bottom of this page.

3. C O N E S

2. X R A Y S | E Y E S

4. R A D I O

5. U L T R A V I O L E T

ACROSS

1. An exploding star will create _____ rays.

2. An _____ will see through your skin right to your bones!

3. Special cells called _____ allow us to see red, green, and blue.

4. _____ stations carry your favorite songs through the air.

5. Butterflies can see _____ light, but humans can't!

6. Electromagnetic _____ waves come in all sizes.

DOWN

7. _____ will heat up your food fast!

8. You could say that your brain sees more than your ____.

9. Snakes have an extra organ that senses _____ light of warm objects.

10. The wavelengths of radiation that humans can see is _____ light.

What determines what you see on the electromagnetic spectrum?

___ ___ ___ ___ ___ ___ ___   ___ ___ ___ ___ ___ ___

Color Confusion

What color are the eyes and mouth on each of these faces?

_____   _____

Riding the Radio Waves

A lot of sounds travel the world in the form of radio waves.

Can you find the pattern by connecting this jumble of letters?

WE	O	TA	TR	SP
US	DI WA	L	ON	AC
	TO	AS	IN	
RA	VE	K	AU	
E	S	TO	TS	E

GENIUS GENUS:
LOGICAL LEADER

Hidden Objects

What do you see in this design? Different brains may see different objects. We found four types of objects. Can you find more?

Use the blank space below the design to draw the objects you see.

GENIUS GENUS:
CREATIVITY CHAMPION

Back for more, I see! You don't give up easily, do you? Hmm ... maybe you're brainier than I thought! Now see if you can find the solutions to these mind-benders!

Decoding RGB

Computers create all the colors of the rainbow by combining red, green, and blue—just like the human eye. But unlike the eye, computers do this by following a set of directions called the hex code, a set of six letters and numbers. The first two digits of the hex code tell the computer how much red to use. The next two are for green, and the last two are for blue.

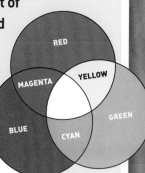

The hex code uses 0123456789ABCDEF to show how much or little of a color exists. 0 is the least and F is the most of a color.

- To create white in hex code, we need to show an absence of red, green, and blue (000000).

- Black uses the full amount of red, green, and blue (FFFFFF).

- To get a color between white and black, we vary the amounts of red, green, and blue.

- A hex of FF00FF creates the color purple because it has no green, but plenty of red and blue.

Here's your challenge, Mastermind: Draw a line matching each hex code with the color it represents.

FF00FF	CYAN
FF9900	GREEN
00FF00	MAGENTA
FFFF00	ORANGE
00FFFF	RED
000099	YELLOW
FF0000	BLUE

GOOD vs. EVIL
Superbrain Showdown

IT'S TIME TO DUKE IT OUT—GENIUS STYLE!

Pit your Mastermind against mine in a Superbrain Showdown. I'll be representing the brainiac baddies of E.V.I.L.; you'll be the champion of those noble noggins of G.O.O.D. You'll face one of these cranium-to-cranium challenges at the end of every chapter.

Use what you learned in this chapter to answer these four questions. If you get them all right, G.O.O.D. wins. But if you don't, E.V.I.L. comes out ahead. So do your best, Mastermind, because I'm about to do my very worst.

You might notice something a little odd about the way each answer choice is labeled. Well, you don't need to worry about that, Mastermind ... not yet, anyway!

1. The portion of light you can see, called _____ **light**, makes up a very small portion of the whole _____ **spectrum**.

| 4. | red, color | 18. | visible, electromagnetic |
| 9. | bright, light | 15. | strobe, disco |

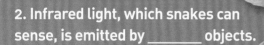

MASTERMIND METER

2. Infrared light, which snakes can sense, is emitted by _____ objects.

23.	fast	5.	warm
21.	bright	12.	silly

3. Cats raised in a world of only vertical lines never learned to see _____.

13. ✓	horizontal lines	6.	other cats
2.	surfaces	15.	dogs

4. How many color receptors do most humans have?

15. ✓	three	14.	twelve
18.	four	21.	sixteen

20% COMPLETE

YOU ARE HERE

RECORD YOUR ANSWERS HERE

1	2	3	4

CHAPTER THREE

Brain-Body Bungles

Feeling smart, Mastermind? Well try this: Lift your hand in the air. Way too easy for your expert egghead, right? But think about what just happened. Your eyes scanned the letters on the page. Your brain interpreted those letters into words and those words into directions. Then your brain signaled thousands of nerves in your arm. Those nerves told dozens of muscles to move. In just the right sequence, groups of muscles stretched longer while others contracted shorter.

All this happened so smoothly and so fast you weren't even aware of it. That's because your body and your brain usually communicate perfectly ... but not always.

In the previous chapter, I showed you how your eyes don't tell you the whole story. Well, they're not the only tricksters. The rest of your body plays tricks on you, too. Want to see how? Turn the page!

Trace all the lines inside the brain without ever lifting your pencil and without tracing the same line twice.

Mental Mistakes

YOUR BODY CONFUSES YOUR BRAIN ALL THE TIME. Usually, you don't notice. But sometimes you can catch it in the act. Check out these four body-brain mind-benders.

SNAP OUT OF IT

SNAP YOUR FINGERS. When your eyes see your fingers snapping and your ears hear the sound, these signals take time to travel to the brain. That means that by the time you observe the snap, it's already happened.

It gets even weirder. Your brain processes sight and sound at different speeds. Yet when you snap your fingers, the motion and the sound seem to happen at the same time. Your brain edits what you observe to make the timing appear perfect. Now that's tricky!

WHO'S THE DUMMY NOW?

Have you ever seen a ventriloquist? This type of performer makes it look like his voice is coming from a dummy. Some people say this slippery entertainer "throws" his voice to perform this trick. But that's impossible!

Here's what's really going on: Your ears hear sound coming from one spot (the ventriloquist's lips), but your eyes see movement in another spot (the dummy's mouth). Your brain puts two and two together and decides that the noise is coming from the dummy. The ventriloquist isn't performing any tricks—though it does take skill to talk while not moving your lips. Your brain actually does most of the work!

EYE DON'T GET IT

Time to test those peepers! Stand in front of a mirror. Then look from one eye to the other several times. Your eyes are moving back and forth, but no matter how hard you try, you can't see the motion. Now watch a friend do the same thing. You can clearly see his eyes moving. What's the deal?

While your eyes are moving back and forth, the image you see should be blurred—think of looking out the window of a moving car. Blurry images are useless, so your brain deletes them and cuts the visual video together so you never notice. Your brain is such an excellent editor that you are none the wiser.

FLOATING ARMS

Stand in a doorway. Move your arms away from your sides and press the backs of your hands against either side of the doorframe. Push up and out as hard as you can, as if you are trying to break the doorway apart. Keep this up for 30 seconds.

Now walk out of the doorway. Try gently lifting your arms out and up. They will seem to float upward on their own, as if they weigh nothing. Weird, huh?

This mental mistake happens because of your brain's ability to tune out sensations. When you pressed your arms against the doorway, your brain gradually got used to the idea that it now takes a lot of effort to hold your arms out. When you stepped out of the doorway and lifted your arms normally, your brain got confused. It reported that your arms were suddenly weightless. Whoops!

Ready for another race to the finish? Put two minutes on the clock and solve these puzzles as fast as you can!

Two letters have been swapped throughout this puzzle (but not the same two letters as in the last chapter!). Unswap the letters to reveal the hidden message.

LETTER **SWAP**

T	H	E	L	O	I	G	E	S	T	H	U	M	A
I	T	O	I	G	U	E	N	I	T	H	E	W	O
R	L	D	N	S	A	L	M	O	S	T	F	O	U
R	N	I	C	H	E	S	F	R	O	M	T	H	E
T	N	P	T	O	T	H	E	T	O	P	L	N	P

___ _____ _____ _____

__ ___ _____ __ _____

____ _____ ____ ___

___ __ ___ ___ ___.

TOTAL TIME TO COMPLETE PUZZLE

This expression is not as hidden as you might think.
Use the hint at the bottom of the page if you need help!

REBUS

WHAT'S THE HIDDEN MESSAGE?

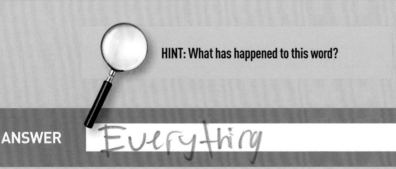

EVERYTHING

HINT: What has happened to this word?

ANSWER Everything

TOTAL TIME TO COMPLETE PUZZLE

Ghost Arm

SOMETIMES, A PERSON'S ARM OR LEG IS SEVERELY DAMAGED.
Doctors may have to perform surgery to remove the limb to save the person. But even though the person's arm or leg is gone, the brain sometimes doesn't get the memo: It thinks the limb is still there. This strange occurrence is called **phantom limb syndrome.**

People with a phantom arm feel like they can bend the missing elbow and wiggle the missing fingers—the same way you feel these sensations when you move your arm. But when they look down, the arm they think they're moving isn't there. Sometimes, the sensations people feel from their phantom limbs are unpleasant. A missing leg may itch nonstop—and there's no way to scratch it. Phantom limbs can even be painful. For example, if someone was in an accident that damaged their arm, the arm can continue to hurt from the injury—even after it's been removed. Because the arm is gone, there's no way to stop the pain.

For a long time, doctors struggled to help people with phantom limb pain. How could they treat a body part that wasn't there? Finally, a brain scientist named V. S. Ramachandran had an idea. What if he could trick the brain of someone with a phantom limb into thinking the missing appendage was back? Would that cure the pain?

Ramachandran tried out his idea on Philip Martinez. Martinez's left arm had been removed after he was in a motorcycle accident. In Martinez's mind, the phantom arm was twisted in a painful position. Because the limb was gone, Martinez couldn't move his arm to ease the pain.

MYTHS BUSTED!

MYTH: Carrots help you see in the dark.

BUSTED!: Carrots contain Vitamin A, which keeps your eyes healthy. But no amount will give the ability to see in the dark.

Ramachandran asked Martinez to place his healthy right arm inside a **mirror box,** a cardboard box with a mirror on one side. Then he asked Martinez to look at the reflection of the right arm and imagine that the reflection was the missing left arm.

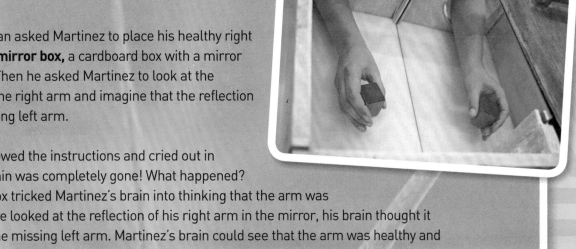

Martinez followed the instructions and cried out in shock. The pain was completely gone! What happened? The mirror box tricked Martinez's brain into thinking that the arm was back. When he looked at the reflection of his right arm in the mirror, his brain thought it was seeing the missing left arm. Martinez's brain could see that the arm was healthy and in a comfortable position. So it stopped creating the feelings of pain that bothered Martinez. Martinez practiced with the mirror box for several weeks, and his phantom pain went away and never came back. All he had to do was trick his brain!

IMA GENIUS'S BRAINIAC BONUS: CONNECTION

The only "connection" these words have is through this puzzle!

Start by placing the word C-O-N-N-E-C-T-I-O-N in the yellow squares. Then prove you're a brainiac by fitting all of the words at right into the grid.

CELLO
EPIC
IGLOO
NACHO
NERVE
NOON
OCEAN
TAXI
TONIC

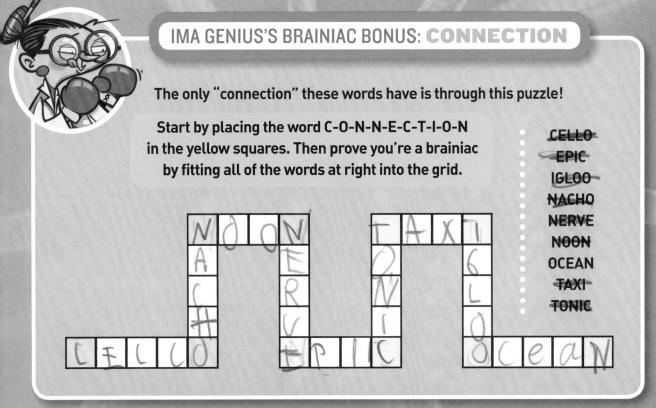

Is your cranium confused yet? Too bad! See if you can figure out the puzzlers on this page.

Line 'Em Up

Which black line is longer?

GENIUS GENUS:
SPATIAL SUPERSTAR

MYTHS
BUSTED!

MYTH: The Great Wall of China can be seen from space.

BUSTED!: Though astronauts have spotted some human-made structures, like the Egyptian pyramids at Giza, the Great Wall isn't visible.

Ambigram

What is this word? Are you sure?
Turn the book upside down and then see what it spells.

This word is an ambigram. Ambigrams are words that retain their meaning when read from a different direction—upside down, in this case. It goes to show you that what's in front of you isn't always as it first appears.

Brain at Work

Did you know that your brain (and not your eyes) does most of the work when you're reading? We've removed all the vowels from this message. If you can determine even part of what the message says, you will have your proof!

PN   SGNLS   TRVL   T   YR   BRN   VRY   SLWLY—   T   JST

TW   FT   PR   SCND.   THT'S   WHY   F   Y   STB   YR   T,

TW   R   THR   SCNDS   PSS   BFR   Y   FL   TH   PN.

SIGNALS TRAVEL TO YOUR BRAIN

The Man Who Sees With His Tongue

ERIK WEIHENMAYER ALWAYS WANTED TO BE A CLIMBER. When he lost his vision at age 13, that dream seemed impossible. But he didn't let blindness stop him. In 2001, he became the first blind person to get to the top of the world's highest mountain—Mount Everest. Today, he scales sheer rock faces, clinging to tiny bumps and crevices to inch his way up. Weihenmayer can't use his eyes to do this—but he can still see.

When Weihenmayer wants to climb, he places a device called the BrainPort in his mouth. Suddenly, he can see the sheer rock face in front of him—with his tongue.

How does it work? BrainPort is a square about the size of a lollipop covered with more than 600 tiny electrodes. Weihenmayer holds it on top of his tongue. He also wears a pair of dark glasses with an attached camera that transmits video to the BrainPort. The BrainPort converts the video image into patterns of electrical pulses that Weihenmayer feels on his tongue. When Weihenmayer first tried the BrainPort, he saw nothing. But after just a few minutes, he could see well enough to reach out and grab a tennis ball rolling in front of him. His brain was learning to translate the patterns of pulses on the tongue to visual images.

This technology seems impossible. But it works because you don't see with your eyes alone. Your brain does most of the seeing. Your eyes take in light and convert it into electrical signals. Your brain reads

those signals as images. Just like your eyes, the BrainPort's video camera takes in light and converts it into electrical signals. It sends these signals to the tongue, and the tongue passes them along to the brain. At first, the brain doesn't speak this new language. But it learns fast. Soon, the brain's visual center can understand the new tongue signals.

The BrainPort isn't perfect—its 611 electrodes can process far less information than a pair of eyes. But Weihenmayer can see well enough to find and pick up a coffee cup on his kitchen counter, play tic-tac-toe, and even play soccer with his daughter. What a brainy invention!

Supersenses

If the brain can learn to see using electrical signals from a camera, what could it do with other kinds of signals? That's what brain scientist David Eagleman wants to know. Eagleman wants to tap into the brain's ability to learn new information to give humans brand-new senses.

Eagleman is creating a vest covered with electrodes, like the BrainPort. He can send the vest all kinds of data, like ultraviolet or infrared light. The vest turns the data into a pattern of vibrations that the wearer feels against the skin. Eagleman thinks that, over time, the brain will learn to make sense of these signals. Using the vest, humans could see ultraviolet energy, like a butterfly, or infrared, like a snake. How would you like to have these superhuman senses?

ATOM'S BRAIN BREAK

Flies and butterflies have taste sensors on their feet.

Mega Mix-Up!

Someone is trying to make this puzzle very hard for you ... I wonder who?

Each row and column has only one picture and one label for ear, eye, hand, arm, and leg, but here is the tricky part: The pictures and labels should NOT match (except for one square).

Complete the boxes and labels to determine which is the only square in the whole puzzle where the label matches the picture.

GENIUS GENUS: LOGICAL LEADER

EAR	_____	_____	HAND	LEG
_____	EYE	HAND	ARM	_____
_____	LEG	EAR	EYE	_____
HAND	_____	ARM	_____	EYE
EYE	HAND	_____	_____	ARM

Circulation

Put these words in order around the picture below (one word per question mark) to learn something very interesting about yourself. Hint: Let the colors be your guide!

BLOOD   A   ARE   THE   VESSELS
          ENOUGH
WRAP   TWO   YOUR   AND   HALF   AROUND
         IN
EARTH   TO   THERE   TIMES
                              MILES
OF   60,000   BODY

GENIUS
GENUS:
WORD
WIZARD

Decoding the Human Body

Have you ever heard of Morse code? It uses a series of short and long signals of light or sound to communicate letters and numbers across long distances. In some ways, Morse code is very similar to how neurons send messages through your body.

Can you decode the message below?

A ·—	J ·———	S ···	1 ·————
B —···	K —·—	T —	2 ··———
C —·—·	L ·—··	U ··—	3 ···——
D —··	M ——	V ···—	4 ····—
E ·	N —·	W ·——	5 ·····
F ··—·	O ———	X —··—	6 —····
G ——·	P ·——·	Y —·——	7 ——···
H ····	Q ——·—	Z ——··	8 ———··
I ··	R ·—·	0 —————	9 ————·

Toy Thief

For more than a month, Alexa and Jack have been tracking a toy thief who stole a rare and valuable stuffed teddy bear. Jack just discovered that the thief has contacted a toy collector and that the two are planning to meet. The thief wants money for the bear. Jack tracked the buyer to an abandoned house on Wella Way, but the buyer was long gone. The house was empty except for an old toy box, an old mirror, and a small desk with one piece of paper on it. Jack looked at the note and said, "Nothing useful here." When Alexa picked up the note, she smiled. "I know where he's selling the bear!"

How did Alexa figure out where the thief will be?

Can you figure out the location?

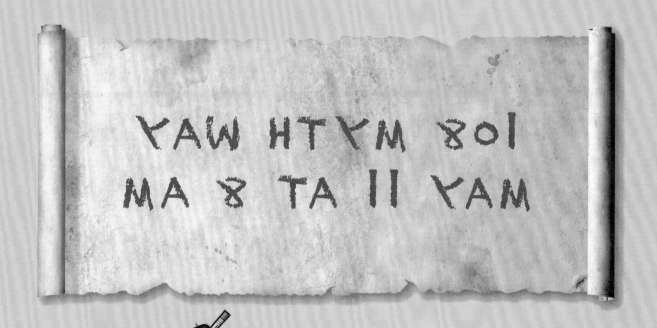

AnyBODY who can solve these puzzles is a true genius! (Ha! I crack myself up.)

GOOD vs. EVIL
Superbrain
Showdown

I HOPE YOU PUT ON YOUR THINKING CAP THIS MORNING, BECAUSE YOU'RE ABOUT TO NEED IT. That's right, it's time for another Superbrain Showdown. See if you can correctly complete this tricky test on the brain-body connection. Answer these four questions with information from the chapter ... if you can!

1. You don't notice when you snap your fingers, but your brain processes _____ and _____ at different speeds.

22.	**sight, sound**	**10.**	**cartoons, jokes**
14.	**red, blue**	**15.**	**TV shows, movies**

MASTERMIND METER

2. V. S. Ramachandran discovered that he could use a device called a _____ to cure phantom limb pain.

4.	pencil	18.	stethoscope
5.	mirror box	7.	carrot peeler

3. The BrainPort converts video into _____ that pulse on the tongue.

1.	electrical signals	2.	numbers
11.	words	13.	tastes

4. Someday, humans could use a special vest to see ultraviolet energy, like a _____ does.

3.	horse	5.	snake
17.	unicorn	12.	butterfly

30% COMPLETE

YOU ARE HERE

RECORD YOUR ANSWERS HERE

1	2	3	4
15	4	11	12

CHAPTER FOUR

Your Hidden Brain

I bet you feel like you know your brain pretty well, right?
Well, I've got a secret: There's a lot more going on in there than you know about.

Confused? Ha! I thought you might be. Here's an example that might help you understand: Did you tie your shoes this morning? I bet you did it in a few seconds flat, right? Now here's the tricky part. Without looking at your laces, try to explain what you did, step by step. Did you start by crossing the right lace over the left? Did you make a loop? What next?

Tying your shoes is so simple you could practically do it in your sleep. So why is this action so hard to explain?

Don't worry—there's nothing wrong with your noggin. It's just that your thinker doesn't always clue you in on every little thing it's up to. Want to learn more about what your brain is up to behind your back? Read on!

Trace all the lines inside the brain without ever lifting your pencil and without tracing the same line twice.

What You Don't Know That You Know

WHEN YOU SWING A BASEBALL BAT OR PLAY AN INSTRUMENT, your **unconscious** controls most of the activity. This is the part of your mind that runs without you knowing about it. Your **conscious** mind, the part that turns on when you wake up in the morning, is mostly left out of the action. Want to learn more? Check out these examples to get a backstage look at your brain!

SECRETS OF **SPORTS** CHAMPIONS

You would probably expect that experts would have extremely high brain activity while performing the feats they're best at. But when people are really good at something, like Shaun White is really good at snowboarding, they stop thinking about what they're doing. Chess masters, athletes, and other superskilled people operate on autopilot—they're "in the zone." They've practiced their moves so many times that, for the most part, they don't have to think about them with their conscious mind. Their unconscious runs the show.

Even if you're not a chess champion or a star athlete, you still have this experience. Think about riding a bike, or playing an instrument ... or tying your shoes. Your unconscious performs all these actions automatically. It's when you overthink things and get your conscious mind involved that you wobble on your bike or fumble the song.

SNAKE **SENSOR**

You're hiking in the mountains when you notice something out of the corner of your eye: a squiggly shape writhing on the ground. You're off like a flash, reacting before you even have a chance to think, SNAKE!

Amazingly, the human brain seems to be wired to sense snakes. Scientists tested this in an experiment by flashing a set of six pictures on a screen. Sometimes, all the pictures were of fruit. Other times, a picture of a snake, a spider, or a mushroom was hiding in the set. Volunteers pressed a button the moment they saw a snake, spider, or mushroom.

When the picture of the snake flashed on the screen, the volunteers were super speedy at pressing the button—much faster than when they saw the spider or the mushroom. What was going on?

Information from our eyes travels to our brain's visual center at the back of our heads. On the way, it passes through an area of the brain called the thalamus. Inside the thalamus is a cluster of neurons that acts like a snake detector. When this cluster senses that you've spotted a snake, it sends a message directly to your muscles—DANGER! GET BACK! This warning system is how we can jump away from a snake before we've even realized what we're looking at.

DECISION-MAKER

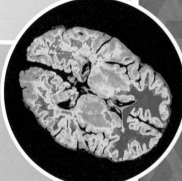

Sometimes, the way your brain works can get a tad, well, spooky. In one experiment, scientists hooked up volunteers up to MRI machines, which measure brain activity. The volunteers had to decide to press one of two buttons and were instructed to let the scientists know the moment they had made a decision about which button to push.

By watching the volunteers' brain activity, the scientists could actually predict which button the volunteers would hit. Amazingly, they could tell *seven* whole seconds before the volunteers said they had made the decision.

This experiment shows that our unconscious minds could be starting to make our choices for us, before our conscious minds chime in. Hey, who's in charge here?

TiME TRiALS

Two letters have been swapped throughout this puzzle (but not the same two letters as in the last chapters!).

Unswap the letters to reveal the hidden message.

LETTER SWAP

T	I	T	A	N	O	B	O	A	E	I	V	L	D
6	0	M	I	E	E	I	O	N	Y	L	A	R	S
A	G	O	I	T	W	A	S	F	I	F	T	Y	F
L	L	T	E	O	N	G	T	H	L	E	O	N	G
L	S	T	S	N	A	K	L	L	V	L	R		

_ _ _ _ _ _ _ _ _ _ _   _ _ _ _ _

_ _   _ _ _ _ _ _ _ _   _ _ _ _ _   _ _ _ .

_ _   _ _ _ _ _   _ _ _ _ _ _   _ _ _ _ _ _ _

_ _ _ _ _ , _ _ _ _   _ _ _ _ _ _ _

_ _ _ _ _ _   _ _ _ _ _ !

TOTAL TIME TO COMPLETE PUZZLE

_ _ : _ _

This is a tough one! See the hint at the bottom of the page if you need help discovering the hidden expression in this rebus!

REBUS

HINT: These words were spoken by an infamous fairy tale queen.

ANSWER

TOTAL TIME TO COMPLETE PUZZLE

Animal Instincts

BEFORE YOU GO GETTING A BIG HEAD ... your brain's hidden abilities aren't so special, humble human. These amazing animals have secret talents so extraordinary you won't believe their brainpower!

MIGRATION MYSTERY

Every fall, tens of millions of monarch butterflies head south for the winter. They fly incredible distances—up to 3,000 miles (4,828 km)—to reach their destinations.

Masses of butterflies travel from the United States and Canada to the same winter roosts each year, clustering on trees in the oyamel fir forests of Mexico. Often, they go to the exact same trees! But here's the most amazing part: Unlike other migrating animals, such as whales, butterflies don't have memories of the trip to help guide them. No single butterfly lives long enough to make the entire round-trip. But somehow, millions find their way. To accomplish their amazing feat, they might use cues from the sun, moon, and stars, or from Earth's magnetic field.

STORM WATCH

In April 2014, a series of 84 tornadoes devastated the southern United States. But the storm was no problem for one group of birds: They got out of the way before it struck.

Two days before the storm hit, a group of golden-winged warblers flew the coop. They flapped 932 miles (1,500 km) over five days to stay out of its path. How did they know? Scientists think they may have been listening in on **infrasonic sounds**—extremely low sounds made by storm systems, earthquakes, and nuclear detonations that can travel long distances. Humans can't hear them, but birds can. Hey, maybe *they* should do the weather report!

DISASTER DETECTORS

Birds aren't the only animals that seem to be able to sense danger on the way.

- Before a giant **tsunami** smashed into Japan in 2011, cats in the affected areas started shaking, becoming agitated, and running away from home.
- As Hurricane Gabrielle moved toward Florida, U.S.A., in 2001, scientists noticed that black-tipped sharks swam away from the coast and into the safety of deeper water.
- In Germany, scientists have noticed strange behavior in red wood ants that build their mounds along **fault lines,** where earthquakes happen. Usually, ants sleep inside their mounds at night. But before an earthquake, the ants keep themselves safe by staying up all night aboveground.

How these creatures sense danger is still a mystery. Scientists think they may get their warnings from infrasonic sound, like the warblers, or maybe they get a clue from tiny weather changes, such as temperature and wind speed shifts.

DOCTOR DOG

Paul Jackson had diabetes. When certain chemicals in his blood got low, he could collapse. But Jackson had a special watchdog—his border collie, Tinker. Jackson noticed that sometimes Tinker would start licking his face, crying, or barking. Soon after, Jackson would pass out. Tinker knew the attacks were coming! With Tinker as a warning system, Jackson could prevent the episodes. Tinker possibly saved his human friend's life—several times!

Tinker did this without any special training, but there are dogs out there that are certified disease detectors. They use their powerful noses, with 50 times more **olfactory,** or smell-sensing, cells than your nose, to sniff out sickness. Other dog doctors can alert their owners of oncoming seizures and even sniff out cancer. Now that's one super sniffer!

Is your cranium confused yet? Too bad! See if you can figure out the puzzlers on this page.

Wordless Search

Budding Geniuses, this is no ordinary word search. In fact, this is a *Wordless* Search. Okay, there are words hidden in this grid, but I'm not telling you what those words are or how many are hidden in there. I'm going to let your unconscious mind find them for you, so if you get stuck, you only have yourself to blame! But because I'm such a nice evil scientist, I *will* tell you that the words may be found forward, backward, up, down, and diagonally—and I'll give you a hint: many of the words are found in this chapter.

D	E	G	N	I	A	R	B
E	P	R	E	D	I	C	T
T	Y	V	E	N	S	E	E
E	A	E	S	O	I	Y	P
C	L	N	U	F	E	U	Y
T	E	N	O	S	U	M	S
O	D	Z	I	S	A	I	U
S	E	C	C	M	E	N	M
E	V	H	S	O	P	D	A
N	C	O	N	T	R	O	L
S	L	I	O	I	E	V	A
E	U	C	C	O	F	S	H
J	E	E	K	N	I	H	T

GENIUS
GENUS:
WORD
WIZARD

Cryptogram

Can you see the hidden message in the code below?

Use the cypher at the bottom of this page to decrypt it.

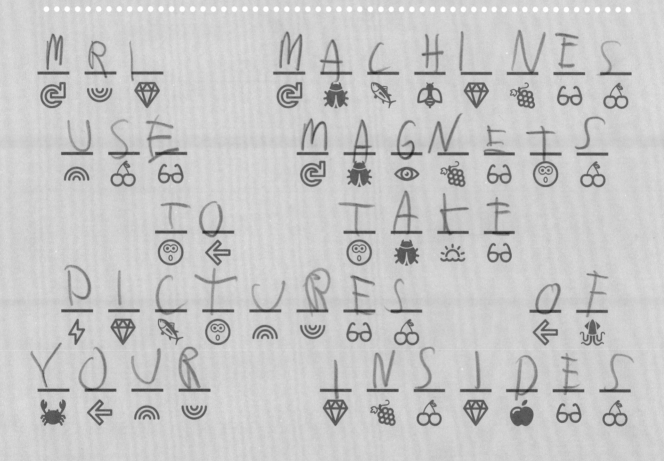

MRI MACHINES
USE MAGNETS
TO TAKE
PICTURES OF
YOUR INSIDES

A	B	C	D	E	F	G	H	I	J	K	L	M

N	O	P	Q	R	S	T	U	V	W	X	Y	Z

The Mystery of the Plane Spotters

IT WAS WORLD WAR II, AND BRITAIN WAS IN TROUBLE. German planes were dropping bombs on towns and villages. To keep people safe, the British needed to devise a way to determine whether the aircraft flying toward them were in fact enemy planes or if they were simply their own troops coming home.

That turned out to be tough to do. It's very difficult to tell faraway airplanes apart, especially when it's nighttime or the sky is cloudy. But the British military quickly determined that there were some people out there with a special talent for identifying planes. These super spotters could glance at an incoming plane and know right away whether it was friend or foe. If it was indeed the enemy approaching, they could warn the military to shoot down the plane before it got close enough to drop its bombs.

These plane spotters were worth their weight in gold. The British army needed more of these eagle-eyed experts, and they wanted to train volunteers. So they asked the plane spotters to explain exactly how they were telling the planes apart: Was it by color? Size? Something about how the planes flew?

The strange thing was that the plane spotters didn't know the answer! They simply looked at the planes and knew what kind they were.

Here's what was going on: Each expert plane spotter's unconscious mind was picking up on tiny details that made one plane different from another. But only the expert's unconscious mind knew what those tiny details were. Their conscious mind was in the dark. That's why the expert spotters couldn't say how they were pulling off their feats of detection.

Eventually, the plane spotters figured out a way to teach their skills—they made training into a guessing game! The trainees would guess whether an incoming plane was a friend or enemy, and the spotter would say whether they were correct. Over time, the trainees became plane-spotting experts, too. Their brains learned to notice tiny details about how the planes looked, flew, or sounded to tell friendly planes from enemy planes ... just like the expert spotters.

This story may seem strange, but you actually engage in this type of learning all the time. When you learn to read, speak a language, ride a bike, or almost anything else, most of the work your brain does is behind the scenes.

ATOM'S **BRAIN BREAK**

Chameleons change color to regulate their temperature or to communicate.

IMA GENIUS'S BRAINIAC BONUS: COUNT ON IT

6	It is time to test your brain by giving you a puzzle without instructions.
6	Have you looked at its name yet?
2	It may help you figure out how to solve it.
3	If you determine the secret I'm hiding, *count* yourself lucky.
5	By all means, use your unconscious mind.
11	Just don't expect me to help you; that's not my job!

—Ima Genius (but are you?)

Spotty Business

PART I

Let's see how you would do as a spotter! Below are the outlines of a few aircraft from World War II, taken from pictures American spotters used to identify aircraft from the ground. First, cover the right-hand page with a piece of paper so it is not visible. Then look over this page for 30 seconds, memorizing as many of the aircraft as you can and whether they are friend or foe. After 30 seconds, remove the cover on the opposite page and place it over this one.

FRIEND

FOE

Here's the hard part, Spotters. Now identify which aircraft are friend or foe by writing "Friend" or "Foe" above the aircraft. And be careful: These aircraft may or may not be pointed in the same direction as when you saw them on the previous page!

PART 2

GENIUS GENUS:
SPATIAL SUPERSTAR

How accurate was your unconscious in identifying the planes, ol' chap? Spotty at best? That's to be expected given the limited time you had! On the other hand, imagine if we had given you a picture of all 537 planes used in WWII!

Not bad, Mastermind. I'm going to have to work a little harder to keep up with you. A *little*.

M. Emery's Mix-Up

It's been one of those days. Four new students registered for Mrs. M. Emery's online class "The Benefits of G.O.O.D. in Society," but the information Mrs. M. Emery received was a jumbled mess. Can you help her unravel the information? She's not sure how old each person is, or which U.S. city he/she lives in. It may help you to remember that names may influence certain qualities about a person. Oh, and Mrs. M. Emery is a rival of Ima's so don't expect Ima to help you with this puzzle!

17	Clinton, CT
18	Dallas, TX
20	Ann Arbor, MI
21	Jasper, TN

GENIUS GENUS: LOGICAL LEADER

STUDENT **Justin Time**
CITY _____
AGE _____

STUDENT **Annie Moment**
CITY _____
AGE _____

STUDENT **Dennis Tree**
CITY _____
AGE _____

STUDENT **Ken D'Corn**
CITY _____
AGE _____

1. The two younger students tend to get things done last minute.
2. Annie is younger than Ken and Dennis, but not Justin.
3. If the four cities are placed in alphabetical order, Ken's city comes right after Annie's and directly before Dennis's.
4. The oldest student lives in CT.
5. The student from CT was named after a popular Halloween treat.

No Manners

Each red letter needs to slide down its column into the correct square (only one letter per square). Some columns have two letters, while others have three. Though the letters appear above the correct columns, they are not necessarily in the right order. The first two boxes have been filled in to help you get started.

The next time your mom or dad says you have no manners, just tell them …

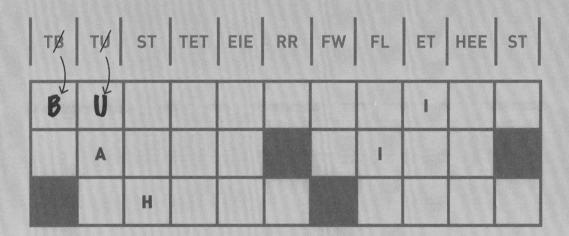

TB	TU	ST	TET	EIE	RR	FW	FL	ET	HEE	ST
B	U							I		
	A						I			
	H									

Riddles

Solving riddles means thinking beyond the obvious. Hey, why don't you get your unconscious mind to help?

1. What has legs but cannot walk, yet leaves to get bigger?

2. How do you stop the sand in an hourglass from running out without flipping the glass to start over?

3. What is at the end of every road?

GOOD vs. EVIL
Superbrain Showdown

ARE YOU READY, MASTERMIND? It's time for the Superbrain Showdown! Are you sure your puny pinhead doesn't need a little nap before you take on my muscular mentality?

Well, don't say I didn't warn you. Put your noggin to the test with these confounding questions. You'd better stretch your skull and warm up your wit, Mastermind. If you get all four right, you beat me!

1. Most of your brain's activity goes on in your _____ mind, the part you're not aware of.

8.	conscious	15.	olfactory
12.	unconscious	3.	sleepy

MASTERMIND METER

2. The brain's _____ gives humans their super snake-sensing ability.

18.	thalamus	11.	auditory cortex
4.	motor cortex	8.	blabber area

3. Birds may know storms are coming because they can hear this type of sound.

6.	ultrasonic	23.	subsonic
5.	infrasonic	16.	tuba

40% COMPLETE

YOU ARE HERE

4. A dog's nose has ____ times more olfactory, or smell-sensing, cells than a human's nose.

4.	fifty	14.	twenty
12.	ten	22.	two

RECORD YOUR ANSWERS HERE

1	2	3	4

CHAPTER FIVE

Memory Mysteries

We humans are memory pack rats. Our brains file away mind-boggling amounts of information—everything from the times tables to the taste of chocolate. Why, I myself can remember the winner of every World Chess Championship since 1886! Hey, why are you laughing?

But even *I* don't remember everything. So how do our brains choose which memories to save? Why are there things you can't seem to remember no matter how hard you try, like the state capitals you need to know for an upcoming test? And why are there other things you can't forget even though you want to, like the time you were the only one who wore your costume to school on Halloween?

These are bona fide memory mysteries, Mastermind. Think you can solve them? Ha! Good luck—even the most eggheaded experts know very little about how to solve these conundrums. Read on for some of brain science's strangest memory stories.

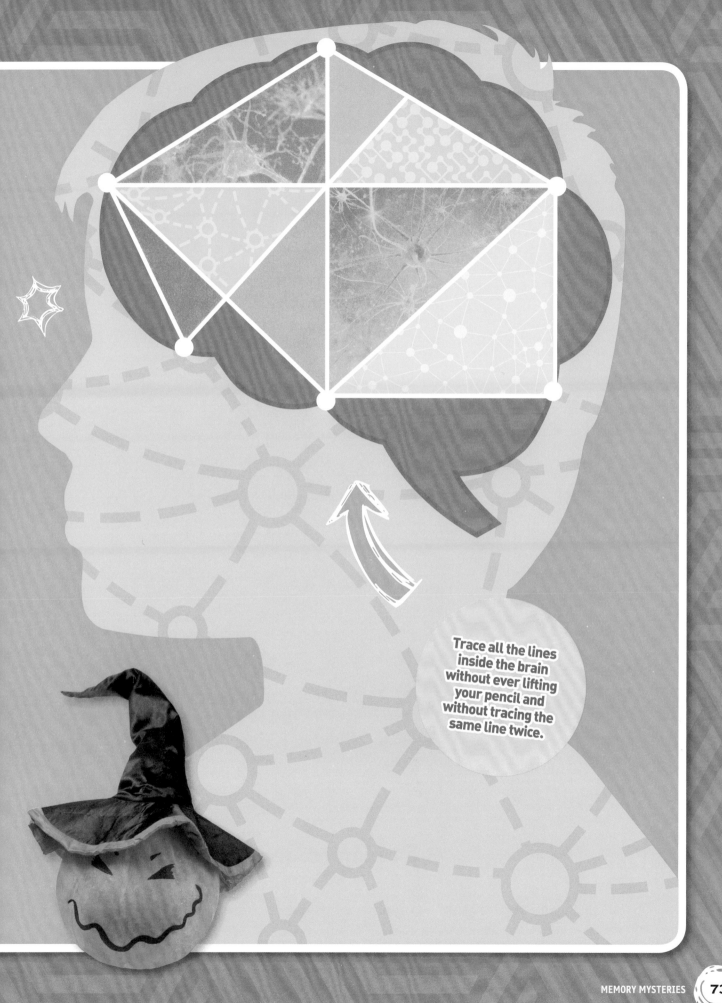

Trace all the lines inside the brain without ever lifting your pencil and without tracing the same line twice.

Memory Face-Off

WHO HAS THE SUPERIOR MEMORY, YOU OR A MOTH?
The answer might surprise you.

HUMAN vs. MOTH

What did you do on your third birthday? If you're like most people, you'll have to ask a family member to find out. Most humans don't have any memories from their first three years. This case of the disappearing memories is called **childhood amnesia.**

Scientists wanted to know more, so they gathered a group of children. When the kids were three years old, the researchers recorded them talking about things they'd been up to recently, like a visit to an amusement park. As the kids got older, the researchers checked in on them to see how much they still remembered from that early time.

At age seven, the children could still recall most of their memories from age three. But when researchers checked back at age eight or nine, these early memories were suddenly gone. That's when childhood amnesia usually hits, and our early memories fade away.

Scientists are still trying to figure out why this happens. They think it might have to do with how our brains change as they grow. For now, it's a memory mystery. All we know is this: For most of us, our first memories disappear forever.

IMA GENIUS'S BRAINIAC BONUS: WHAT'S YOUR NUMBER?

Ima's great-aunt Rebel doesn't have a smartphone; instead, she uses a flip phone to text. To text on a flip phone, she has to use the number pad for letters—kind of like the one pictured at left.

Can you decode the message she recently sent to Ima?

• •

**4 F68N3 96U7 539S. Y68
5EF8 8H36 46 T43 7I2N6.**

A caterpillar scoots along, munching on leaves, until one day it weaves itself a cocoon. When it comes out, it is totally different. The caterpillar has transformed itself into a beautiful butterfly or moth.

But have you ever wondered what happens inside that cocoon? You might think the bug starts growing wings. But the truth is that when it enters the cocoon … it melts into goo! From the ooze grows a brand-new creature.

That made scientists wonder: Does a moth remember its past life as a caterpillar? To find out, they trained hornworm caterpillars to dislike a certain smell by giving them a small electric shock each time the crawly creatures got a whiff. Soon, the caterpillars had learned to turn away each time they smelled the odor.

Then it came time for the caterpillars to transform. They entered their cocoons and emerged as moths one month later. It was time for the big test. The researchers gave the moths a whiff of the odor and … they hated it! They remembered what they had learned as caterpillars and turned away. Even though the caterpillars' bodies had turned into goo, somehow their memories survived.

You didn't think I'd forget about the Time Trials, did you? Nice try, Mastermind.

Two letters have been swapped throughout this puzzle (but not necessarily the same two letters as in the last chapters!)
Unswap the letters to reveal the hidden message.

LETTER **SWAP**

N	O	E	G	T	E	E	I	N	G	T	N	O	U
G	H	S	L	T	T	P	C	A	N	M	A	K	T
Y	O	U	R	T	M	T	M	B	T	R	E	H	I
N	G	S	E	H	A	E	D	I	D	N	O	E	A
C	E	U	A	L	L	Y	H	A	P	P	T	N	

_____ _____ _____

_____ ____ ___ ____

___ _____ ____

____ ___ ___ _

_____ _____.

TOTAL TIME TO COMPLETE PUZZLE

See the hint at the bottom of the page if you need help discovering
the hidden expression in this rebus!

REBUS

AWAY

 HINT: Consider what is happening to the word.

ANSWER

TOTAL TIME TO
COMPLETE PUZZLE

Memory Masters

JUST BECAUSE I CAN'T REMEMBER WHERE I HID THAT BONE doesn't mean that *all* animals have measly memories. Check out these four amazing critters with awesome recall.

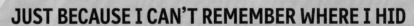

I'M NOT **LION** TO YOU

If I taught you a game right now, do you think you'd remember how to play it in 10 years? That's a pretty tricky task for most humans, whose long-term memories tend to fade over time. But sea lions don't have this problem.

Trainers taught a sea lion named Rio a game. They showed her cards with different symbols on them. If she pointed out the matching pairs, she got a fish. Ten years later, they gave her the test again—and Rio aced it. That gives Rio the longest memory of any creature scientists have tested. I wonder if she could tell me where I buried my bone....

PACHYDERM POWER

How many friends can you pay attention to at once? Most humans can keep track of about three or four other people at a time. Elephants, however, can keep tabs on about 30 other elephants in their herd. It doesn't matter where they are or how far away.

How do they do it? Elephants create a mental map of their herdmates ... using pee! Every time an elephant comes across urine from a herdmate, it takes note of that elephant's size and what direction it was going. This information helps these big brainiacs remember what all their friends are up to.

EIGHT-LEGGED EINSTEIN

How would you like to flip through your math book the night before a test and remember everything in it? If you had an octopus's brain, you might be able to.

In humans, **short-term memories** (like the phone number you hold in your head for a few seconds while you dial) and **long-term memories** (like how to ride a bike) are stored in different places. But octopuses are different: Their short-term memories and long-term memories work together. Some scientists think this setup gives octopuses a brainpower boost. Cool trick!

BIRDBRAIN

Do you know where your backpack is right now? What about your shoes? What about ... every single pen and pencil in your house? That last one probably stumped you. But if you were a Clark's nutcracker, a type of bird, you would have no problem with that puzzler.

A Clark's nutcracker can remember the exact location of 30,000 pine nuts. (In comparison, you humans can hold only seven digits in your short-term memory.) The bird spends all fall gathering pine nuts and hiding them. Then winter comes, and snow covers everything. But the nutcracker has no trouble remembering where to dig up a snack whenever it gets hungry.

On top of that, the Clark's nutcracker's **hippocampus** (an area of the brain devoted to memory) keeps getting stronger as it ages. So while human memory usually weakens over time, the memory of a Clark's nutcracker keeps getting better. Who exactly is the birdbrain here?

Think you've got a stronger memory than me, Mastermind? Ha! I can't remember the last time I laughed so hard! Try your hand at these puzzles and we'll see who has the more remarkable recall.

Memory Munch

Time to test your short-term memory! You will need 20 coins the size of a penny or larger (you can also use buttons, pieces of paper, or other objects) to cover the leaves and caterpillars below. Before you cover up the pictures, try to memorize where the caterpillars and leaves are.

Have you covered all the pictures? Great! Time to feed the caterpillars!

Remove one of your coins. If you reveal a caterpillar, find the same color leaf on your next move. If it's a leaf, find the same color caterpillar. If you fail, cover up both pictures and start again. Only leave the coins off if you make a match.

Find That Memory

You have some memories hidden deep in your hippocampus. Can you find your way through months and years of facts, images, and thoughts to find a particular memory?

Move north, south, west, or east (or SW, NW, NE, SE) according to the direction under each space below. When you land on a letter, write the letter down on the space provided. A move of "1E, 2S" means you should move 1 letter East, then 2 South. We've completed the first move for you by starting at the L and moving 1E, 2S to the letter C. You will start at the letter C. Each move starts where the last move ended!

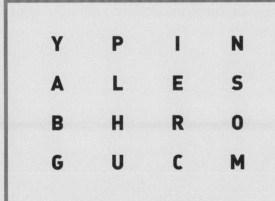

```
Y    P    I    N

A    L    E    S

B    H    R    O

G    U    C    M
```

C __ __ __ __ __ __ __   __ __ __ __
   1E, 2S 1W, 2N 2E, 1S 1N 1NW 1E 3S, 3W   3N 2S, 3E 1S, 2W 1E, 1N

__ __ __ __   __ __ __   __ __ __ __
1N 1N, 2W 2E, 1S 1E   2S, 1W 2N, 2W 3E, 1N   2SW 1NE 1W 1N

__ __ __   __ __ __ __ __ __ __ __
1W 2SE, 1E 1S, 2W   1NE 1N 1E, 2S 2N, 1W 1SE, 1S 3W, 1N 1E, 1NE 1S

Could You Be a Memory Champion?

WELCOME TO THE U.S.A. MEMORY CHAMPIONSHIP. YOU ARE ONE OF THE FINALISTS. THESE ARE YOUR TASKS.

You have 15 minutes to memorize a list of 200 random words, in order. Then you have another 15 minutes to memorize facts about six different people, such as their address, three favorite hobbies, and the make, model, year, and color of their favorite car. Finally, you have five minutes to memorize the order of two decks of shuffled playing cards.

Sounds impossible, right? But the U.S.A. Memory Championship is a real contest held every year in New York City. Those are the real challenges of the championship round. How do the winners accomplish these incredible memory feats?

To find out, scientists from England's University College London gave mental tests to ten champions. The result? Their brilliant brains were actually just average.

But the researchers did discover something interesting. Using brain-scanning technology, they peeked inside the champions' heads as they memorized a set of images. They saw a lot of activity in the part of the brain devoted to spatial memory, the type of memory that you use when you picture where you left your backpack.

Most people don't use this part of the brain to remember things. But spatial memories are powerful, and memory champions know that. They take advantage of their spatial memory's strength with the "memory palace" technique.

Say a champion has a sting of random words to memorize. Using a familiar place as her memory palace, such as her house, she places the words in specific locations inside. When she needs to recall the images, she simply walks through her memory palace. The funnier or weirder the images, the easier they are to remember. Now try it yourself with the challenge at right!

Memory Challenge

If you had to remember a list of unrelated words such as "squirrel," "tennis," and "banana," how would you do it? You might create a crazy story that goes something like this ...

- You find a squirrel sitting on your front steps, eating nuts and getting the shells all over the place.
- Next, you imagine walking into a palace and seeing tennis superstar Serena Williams in your entryway, smacking a serve and smashing a hole in the wall.
- Then, as you enter your living room, you see a giant gorilla sitting on your coffee table, eating bananas and throwing the peels on the floor.

When you need to recall the words, you just walk through your palace: squirrel, tennis, banana.

Try It Yourself

Using the memory palace technique, see if you can memorize this list of random words. The stranger and more hilarious your mental images, the more easily you'll remember them.

1. FAIRY
2. JAM
3. KANGAROO
4. NOODLE
5. HAIR
6. CASTLE
7. EAR
8. TIGER
9. JACKET
10. DUCK

FUNFACT

In 2015, Lance Tschirhart became the first person to memorize a deck of cards in less than 30 seconds.

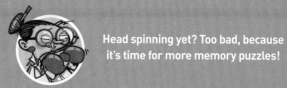

Head spinning yet? Too bad, because it's time for more memory puzzles!

Total Recall

Let's see how well you can recall what you've learned so far.

Use the hints to construct the words in the squares. Then unscramble the yellow squares for a word that ties everything together.

Area that controls memory

☐☐☐☐☐ **+** ☐☐☐☐ **+** ☐☐

Type of memory that helps you memorize a phone number

☐☐☐☐☐   ☐☐☐☐

The point in childhood when childhood amnesia strikes

☐☐☐☐☐

ADDITIONAL HINTS:

"River horse" (deadliest animal on Earth)
A fun summer retreat for kids
Abbreviation for "America"
Opposite of long
Another way of saying "period of time"
Opposite of late

What ties everything together? ☐☐☐☐☐☐

A Place For Everything

What did the Brain say to the Hippocampus?

(Use the hints below to fill in the grid and find the answer to the riddle!)

		H				
			░	░	T	
		O				

T always comes before H

O is always followed by R

K only appears above a T

An S ends the first and third rows

Second H has an E to the right and under

TOE can be found going down

AN comes before K

One E has M to the left and right

IF you only had the last two letters, you would be done.

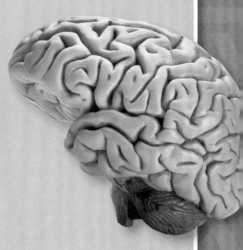

Wow, you sure seem to remember how to use your noggin, Mastermind! Try these tricky tests next.

Word Switch

GENIUS GENUS:
WORD WIZARD

Are you ready for another memory test? This is an easy one (or is it?).

Take 30 seconds to memorize this list of word switches:

Giraffe = Fence
Flower = Ball
Hamburger = Bike
Lion = Kite
Worms = Water

Now read the passage below, WITHOUT looking back at the list of word switches!

(Remembering those word switches while following the story might not be as easy as I hinted!)

A dog named Jack loved to play outside with a flower. His buddy Terri tossed his flower too far and it soared over the giraffe. When Jack went around the giraffe, he couldn't find the flower, but he spotted a lion flying through the air. A boy was zipping down the street on his hamburger while holding onto the string of the lion. Jack chased the hamburger and the lion. The boy on the hamburger suddenly stopped. The lion floated down and landed on the giraffe. And right below it, Jack spotted another flower. He scooped up the flower, slipped through the hole in the giraffe, and headed home. Jack had enjoyed chasing the flower, hamburger, and lion, but he had a nice cold bowl of worms waiting for him at home.

Shape That Memory

How good are you at memorizing shapes? How fast are you at finding the shape when it is hidden among similar shapes?

Determine the number of times the shape at right appears below.

Keep in mind (seriously, keep the shape in your mind!), this shape can be rotated, but not flipped.

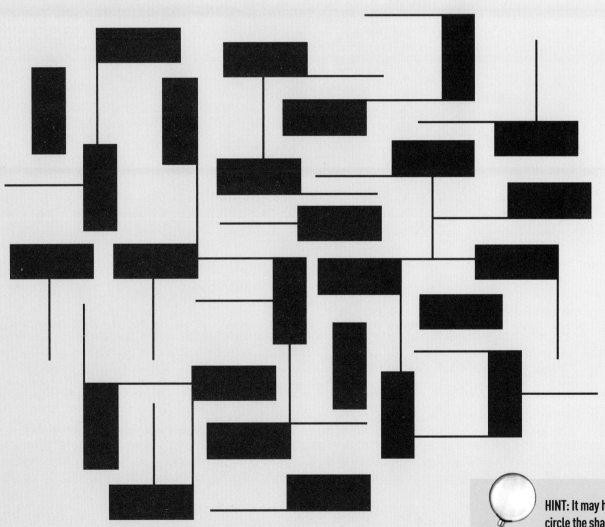

HINT: It may help you to circle the shape when you find it.

GOOD vs. EVIL
Superbrain Showdown

BACK FOR MORE, I SEE! Guess you couldn't *remember* who the champ is here. Maybe you need me to remind you.

It's time to go noggin-to-noggin in another Superbrain Showdown. I hope you like the classroom, Mastermind, because you're about to get schooled!

1. Most people have no memories from before they turned three. This phenomenon is called _____.

4. forgotten childhood	23. disappearing memory syndrome
1. childhood amnesia	11. forgetfulitis

2. The _____ area of the brain is devoted to memory. In a Clark's nutcracker, it gets stronger as the bird ages.

14.	hippocampus	**16.**	motor cortex
5.	olfactory cortex	**26.**	rememberocortex

3. When you look up a phone number and hold it in your mind for a few seconds while you reach for the phone, you're using your _____.

24.	long-term memory	**10.**	spatial memory
4.	short-term memory	**3.**	phone number memory

4. Humans have strong _____ memories, which help us visualize where things are. To take advantage of this ability, competitive memory champions use a technique called the _____.

1. ~~childhood, childhood amnesia~~

16. pack rat, octopus brain boost

7. spatial, memory palace

6. false, house of lies

50% COMPLETE

YOU ARE HERE

RECORD YOUR ANSWERS HERE

1	2	3	4

CHAPTER SIX

Brain Buddies

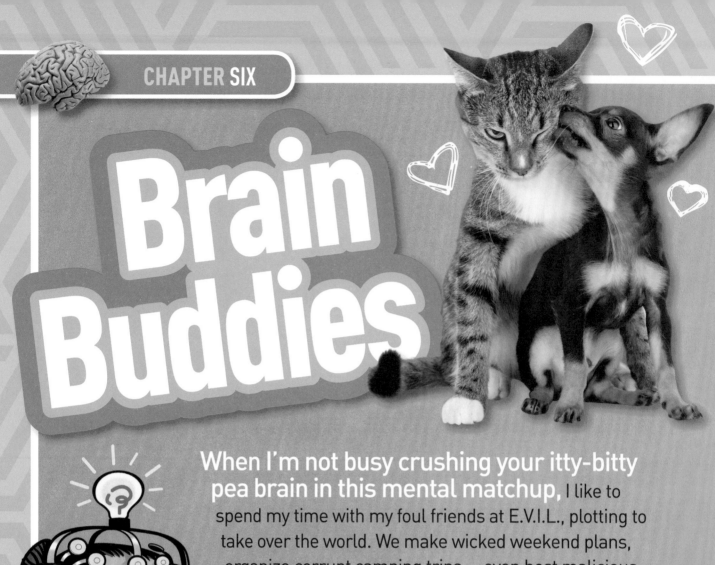

When I'm not busy crushing your itty-bitty pea brain in this mental matchup, I like to spend my time with my foul friends at E.V.I.L., plotting to take over the world. We make wicked weekend plans, organize corrupt camping trips ... even host malicious TV marathons. It's a blast!

You and your friends might spend your time going to the movies instead of scheming global domination. But whether your brain works for G.O.O.D. or E.V.I.L., you probably spend a lot of time socializing with your pals.

Our brains are wired to buddy up. Whether it's with our friends, our family members, or even our pets, we like to have other noggins around. But why? Read on to learn some surprising science about your social smarts.

Trace all the lines inside the brain without ever lifting your pencil and without tracing the same line twice.

Cranial Companionship

YOUR FRIENDS AND FAMILY AREN'T IMPORTANT ONLY TO YOU; they're a big deal to your noggin, too. Your buddies change your brain in ways you've probably never considered. Check out these examples.

SOCIAL SKULLS

When a friend is going through tough times, do you ever say "I know how you feel"? It's not just an expression. Humans have **empathy,** the ability to share the feelings of other people. A 2013 study showed how this skill works in our brains.

Scientists assembled a group of people and ran brain scans on them. While participants were in the scanner, the scientists told them that they might get an electric shock. Fear of that possibility made certain parts of their brains light up. When the scientists then told the subjects that a stranger might get a shock, those same brain regions were silent.

Amazingly, though, when the scientists told the participants that a *friend* of theirs might get a shock, their brains lit up just like they did when they themselves felt threatened!

It seems that when our friends are in danger, we may feel as if we are in danger, too. As far as our brains are concerned, the people we're close to are part of ourselves. Now that's some sappy science!

RELATED RELATIONSHIPS

We all know that good friends feel like family. A 2014 study shows that there might be a reason for that. Scientists found that friends have more of the same **genes** than strangers do. (Genes are the parts of your cells that carry information about how you look and behave.)

The scientists tested the genes of almost 2,000 people. They found that people's friends are as closely related to them as fourth cousins. That's the same thing as having the same great-great-great-grandparent as your best buddy!

Health Helper

Scientists found that people with lots of social relationships are less likely to catch colds. They did this by gathering a group of people. First, they counted how many social relationships each person had. Then they infected the participants with a cold virus and waited to see who would get sick. (They weren't evil scientists—the people volunteered.)

The researchers found that the more friends the volunteers had, the better they were at fighting off the virus. More than 60 percent of people with just a few social relationships came down with a cold. But only 35 percent of people with a lot of social relationships got sick. The bonds of friendship can help keep us healthy, and that's nothing to sneeze at!

MYTHS BUSTED!

MYTH: Touching a baby bird will make its parents reject it.

BUSTED!: Birds can't smell well enough to tell if humans have been around their young. But disturbing a nest may make them abandon it, so hands off!

TiME TRiALS

Ready to see whose brain has superior speed? See if you can solve these puzzles in less than two minutes!

Two letters have been swapped throughout this puzzle (but not necessarily the same two letters as in the last chapters!). Unswap the letters to reveal the hidden message.

LETTER SWAP

O	N	F	V	E	R	F	G	E	F	P	E	R	S
O	N	M	F	K	E	S	3	9	6	A	R	I	E
N	D	S	I	N	F	L	I	A	E	T	I	M	E
S	I	X	O	A	T	H	O	S	E	W	I	L	L
B	E	B	E	S	T	A	R	I	E	N	D	S

___ _____, _ _____

_____ ___

_____ __ _

_____. ___

___ _____ ____

__ ____ _____.

TOTAL TIME TO COMPLETE PUZZLE

See the hint at the bottom of the page if you need help discovering the hidden expression in this rebus!

REBUS

YES

HINT: Say both items together out loud.

ANSWER

TOTAL TIME TO COMPLETE PUZZLE

Do Animals Have Friendships?

FOR A LONG TIME, SCIENTISTS THOUGHT that having friendships was one of the ways humans were different from other animals. They didn't consider that other creatures could have long-lasting and important relationships, too. Silly scientists! Check out these beastly buds that prove them wrong.

FOOD OR FRIENDSHIP

You humans like to think that we animals will do anything for food. (And, I'll admit, I *really* like my treats.) But the results of this study might surprise you!

First, scientists created a box with a transparent divider in the middle. They placed a rat on each side. One of the rats was forced to swim in a pool of water— something rats really hate. The only way it could escape to dry land was if the second rat pushed open a small door connecting the two sides.

Once the rats learned how to open the door, they regularly opened it to help out their soaked buddy. *Awww!* But then the scientists made it trickier. They had the rat on the dry side choose between two doors: One was the door that allowed the rat's companion to escape the water; behind the other was a yummy chocolate snack. Even when tempted by the treat, the rats most often chose to help their companions before snagging the snack. How sweet!

HORSING AROUND

Studies seem to show that, whether human or animal, friendships can help keep us healthy. But are friendships essential to some species' very survival?

To find out, scientists studied a group of 400 wild horses in New Zealand. By noting which horses

PAGING DR. MONKEY

Off the coast of Puerto Rico, there is a small island nicknamed "Island of the Monkeys." No humans live there—just hundreds of rhesus monkeys. Biologist Lauren Brent spent four years studying one group of them.

Brent wanted to find a way to measure the effect of monkey friendships. She wondered if having more friends would lower the monkeys' stress levels. So she measured their **glucocorticoid** levels. Glucocorticoid is a chemical the body produces when it feels stressed. She did this by collecting the monkeys' poop and testing it for the chemical.

Brent found that the more friends a monkey had, the lower its stress level. Just like human friendships, monkey friendships help keep these creatures happy and healthy. That's no monkey business!

played together and groomed each other with their teeth, they figured out how many friends each horse had.

The scientists noticed that the horses with a lot of friends raised a lot of foals. Friendships seemed to support the mares so that they gave birth to more young, enabling the herd to thrive for many generations into the future.

DEVOTED DOLPHINS

Many animals seem to like hanging around each other. But are their friendships deep bonds on the level of human friendships? That's a hard question to answer. Dolphins, however, might give us a clue.

Dolphins use lots of sounds to communicate, including chirps and whistles. Then there are **signature whistles.** Dolphins' signature whistles are like their names—each dolphin has its own unique one. When a dolphin swims up to a group of unfamiliar dolphins, it introduces itself with its signature whistle. And dolphins call each other by their signature whistles, just like humans use each other's names when they're talking.

One scientist took a look at 43 different dolphins in zoos across the nation. Using underwater speakers, he played them recordings of dolphins that used to share their tanks. When he played the signature whistle of a dolphin that hadn't been around for a long time, the dolphin he was studying would often come up to the speakers, look at them intently, and whistle at them. They didn't act this way when he played signature whistles of dolphins they had never met. The scientist found that dolphins can remember the signature whistles of their old tankmates after being separated for more than 20 years. Now that's loyal friendship!

Healthy Living

**GENIUS
GENUS:**
CREATIVITY
CHAMPION

We're not giving you directions for this puzzle!
If you're stuck, ask a few friends for help.

HAVING A _____ _____ OF _____ COULD HELP YOU LIVE LONGER.

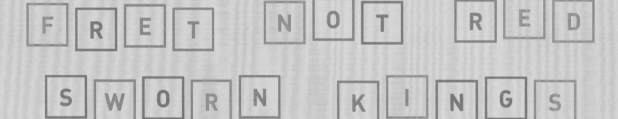

| F | R | E | T | | N | O | T | | R | E | D |

| S | W | O | R | N | | K | I | N | G | S |

Missing Friend

Complete the
pattern. Hint: A
right-facing
dolphin is the key
to figuring out the
missing piece.

Friendship Points

There are 90 words that can be created from the letters in "FRIENDSHIP" that have five or more letters and that don't end in the letter *S*.

List as many as you can below.

If you score at least 35 points, you are a Genius!
If you score 24–34 points, you are a Genius-in-Training! Give yourself
3 bonus points for each friend or family member you ask to help.

5-Letter Words
(1 point each)

1. _____
2. _____
3. _____
4. _____
5. _____
6. _____
7. _____
8. _____
9. _____
10. _____
11. _____
12. _____
13. _____
14. _____
15. _____

6-Letter Words
(2 points each)

1. _____
2. _____
3. _____
4. _____
5. _____
6. _____
7. _____
8. _____
9. _____
10. _____
11. _____
12. _____
13. _____
14. _____
15. _____

7-Letter Words
(4 points each)

1. _____
2. _____
3. _____
4. _____
5. _____
6. _____
7. _____
8. _____
9. _____
10. _____

8-Letter Words
(5 points each)

1. _____
2. _____
3. _____
4. _____
5. _____

Friends/relatives I asked for help:

_____

TOTAL POINTS [   ]

Grab a buddy, because you might need the power of two brains to solve these tricky brain tests.

Follow the Crowd

IMAGINE THAT YOU'RE WAITING FOR AN ELEVATOR. The car arrives, the bell dings, and the doors open. You join four other people inside the elevator. While you're riding, they do something strange—they all turn around and face the rear! What do you do?

You might think that you'd ignore the silly behavior of your elevator companions and keep facing forward. But you're probably wrong. The first reality TV show, *Candid Camera*, secretly filmed people in this same situation in 1962. Nearly every person turned to face the same way as their backward companions.

Our social brains make us want to fit in. We **conform,** or act like those around us, to be part of the group. Think about it: Groups of friends tend to dress in similar clothes, speak alike, and share the same likes and dislikes.

This drive helps us work together. It makes groups of humans a powerful force, enabling armies to conquer and sports teams to take the gold. But as the elevator experiment shows, sometimes we act like everyone else even when it's just plain silly.

Consider an experiment by psychologist Solomon Asch in 1955. Asch put seven men together in a room. Only one was an actual volunteer; the rest were actors just *pretending* to be volunteers. Asch showed the men two cards. Card 1 had one line on it; Card 2 had three lines of different lengths on it. Asch went around the table from person to person and asked, "Which line on Card 2 is the same length as the line on Card 1?"

The correct answer was obvious. But the six actors had been instructed to pick the wrong line. One by one, they chose a line on Card 2 that was either much too short or much too long. Then it was the subject's turn. Even though it was clear that everyone else was wrong, he almost always agreed with the group and picked one of the wrong lines. Only 25 percent of the people tested chose the right answer.

This experiment shows that we have such a strong drive to follow the crowd that we'll do it even when we know the crowd is wrong. But just because a group is acting a certain way doesn't mean you should, too.

Let that be a lesson to you, Mastermind. Don't be afraid to think for yourself!

IMA GENIUS'S BRAINIAC BONUS: TWO OF A KIND

What did one chromosome say to his friend?

(Because I'm such a generous genius, I'll give you brainiacs a hint: The number before a letter tells you how many times that letter occurs in the puzzle. Start with the letter E.)

7E 2R 2W 1T 2N 2G 3A 1M 2S

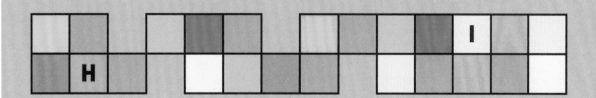

Whew, you've been giving me quite the mental workout, Mastermind. But I bet these puzzles will prove too tricky for you!

Mastermind Network

Have you ever met someone only to find out you share a friend in common? If you have a particular person you want to meet, you may find that a friend of a friend of a friend knows that person! Below is a picture of the Mastermind Network. Each square represents a person, and the lines connect people who know each other. In which *empty* square should you place your name to give you access to Ima, Atom, Ima's great-aunt Rebel and Mrs. M. Emery so that you are no more than three connections away from each of them?

Remember: A connection is a single move from one square to the next. Do not jump from line to line where they intersect.

GENIUS GENUS:
LOGICAL LEADER

Great-Aunt Rebel

Mrs. M. Emery

Amazing Choice

Do you prefer to conform or to think for yourself? Navigate this unusual maze and see which word(s) you come closer to on your way to the star.

There are four possible ways into the maze—one in each of its corners. Most people enter at one of the two openings on the bottom.

Genius Advice

No, this isn't a pizza, my genius wannabes. This is a letter wheel.
Place each missing letter in the correct spot to get some "independent" advice.

MISSING LETTERS: E I O O U

Non conformist

The Johnson octuplets often play tricks on people by dressing alike.

Can you spot the one who likes to stand out?

GOOD vs. EVIL
Superbrain Showdown

HERE WE GO, MASTERMIND. IT'S TIME FOR OUR BULKED-UP BRAINS TO DUKE IT OUT IN ANOTHER SUPERBRAIN SHOWDOWN. If you get all four questions right, G.O.O.D. wins. If not, E.V.I.L. prevails. So, no pressure ... MUAHAHA!

1. Which of the following is true?

17. When a friend is in danger, your brain has activity in the same areas as when you are in danger.

4. The more friends you have, the less likely you are to get sick.

15. You and your friends may be as closely related as fourth cousins.

18. all of the above

MASTERMIND METER

2. Just as human acquaintances use names to refer to each other, dolphins use _____ to refer to their friends.

5.	signature whistles	13.	name tags
24.	bubbles	7.	chirps

3. Which of the following is NOT true?

6. ✓ Monkeys with strong friendships are less stressed.

2. Horses with strong friendships raise more foals.

3. Dolphins remember friends they haven't seen for 20 years.

5. Rats always choose food over friendship.

YOU ARE HERE

60% COMPLETE

4. Solomon Asch's 1955 experiment showed that ...

15. people don't listen to those around them.

4. people like to stand out from the crowd.

14. people will choose an incorrect answer just because other people do.

22. ✓ elevators can be dangerous.

RECORD YOUR ANSWERS HERE

1	2	3	4
18 4	✓ 5	6	14 22

Talking Heads

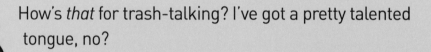

What's that you're saying? You think you can beat me in this battle of the brainiacs? Ha! Good luck. Why, I've barely begun to unleash the full power of my noggin on your teensy thinker. Your brain is so weak, it thinks the periodic table is a piece of furniture!

How's *that* for trash-talking? I've got a pretty talented tongue, no?

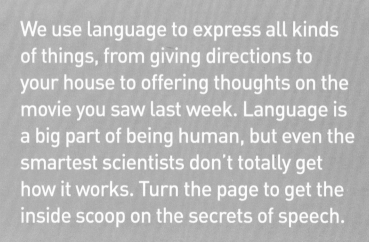

We use language to express all kinds of things, from giving directions to your house to offering thoughts on the movie you saw last week. Language is a big part of being human, but even the smartest scientists don't totally get how it works. Turn the page to get the inside scoop on the secrets of speech.

Trace all the lines inside the brain without ever lifting your pencil and without tracing the same line twice.

Wise Words

ALL OVER THE WORLD, PEOPLE CHAT about how their day went, what they want to eat for dinner, and what they're going to do over the weekend. Incredibly, there are as many as 7,000 languages spoken worldwide! Even in the same language, people use different words to describe the same things. That made scientists wonder: Can the language you speak affect the way you think?

COLOR CHAT

Do we understand colors with our eyes ... or is it all in our heads? In a 1954 study, scientists found that the Zuni people of the southwestern United States—whose language does not have separate words for the colors orange and yellow—have trouble telling the two colors apart.

Then there are Russian speakers. When describing something blue, they have to choose between two words: *goluboy* and *siniy*. Could this make them better at telling the difference between shades of blue than people whose language has just one word for the color? In 2007, scientists showed both Russian and English speakers slightly different shades of blue and tested how quickly they could tell them apart. The Russians were 10 percent faster at the task. Color me impressed!

FINDING FAULT

English speakers usually describe an accident by saying who did what—"Sally broke the picture," for example. But in Spanish or Japanese, someone describing the same event would likely say, "The picture broke itself."

A scientist named Caitlin Fausey wanted to see if this language difference changed how people remembered events. She showed people who spoke English, Spanish, and Japanese videos of people popping balloons, breaking eggs, and spilling drinks. Sometimes the people in the videos did it on purpose; other times, it was an accident.

Then, Fausey quizzed her subjects: Can you remember who was responsible for each event? She found that when it was an accident, the Spanish and Japanese speakers did not remember the person who caused the accident as well as the English speakers.

DIRECTIONAL DIALOGUE

The people who live in Pormpuraaw, a remote community in Australia, don't use the words "left" or "right." Instead, they use directions such as "north" and "south." Instead of saying, "Turn left at the big tree," they might say, "Turn east at the big tree." And instead of saying, "You have something on your right arm" they would say, "You have something on your northeast arm."

Because of this directionally different way of speaking, it's nearly impossible to have a conversation in Pormpuraaw unless you know exactly what direction everything is. This means that the people who live there are amazingly good at keeping track of where they are. They always know which way is which, even when they're in new and unfamiliar places. Now that's some smart speech!

IMA GENIUS'S BRAINIAC BONUS: TRANSLATION TIME

What is the name of this famous nursery rhyme?

Bilagy, werafy, fekk.
The igst plon up the sdfgg.
The sdfgg struck one,
The igst plon down,
Bilagy, werafy, fekk.

Grab your pencil and put two minutes on the clock. It's time for another test of your skull's speedy skills. Can you finish these puzzles before the clock runs out?

Two letters have been swapped throughout this puzzle (but not necessarily the same two letters as in the last chapters!).
Unswap the letters to reveal the hidden message.

LETTER **SWAP**

A	H	E	O	F	F	I	C	I	T	L	L	T
N	G	U	T	G	E	O	F	C	T	M	B	O
D	I	T	K	H	M	E	R	H	T	S	A	H
E	L	O	N	G	E	S	A	T	L	P	H	T
B	E	A	7	4	L	E	A	A	E	R	S

___ _____
_____ __
_____, _____,
___ _____
_____—___
_____.

TOTAL TIME TO COMPLETE PUZZLE

See the hint at the bottom of the page if you need help discovering the hidden expression in this rebus!

REBUS

S
T
R
A
MID I DLE
G
H
T

HINT: Start with the vertical word; what's it doing to the horizontal word?

ANSWER

TOTAL TIME TO
COMPLETE PUZZLE

☆

Translation Face-Off

IT WOULD BE NICE IF YOU KNEW JUST WHAT YOUR DOG WAS THINKING. (I'll give you a hint: It's usually *FEED ME!*) What if animals could actually talk to people? And what if humans could talk back? Let's open up some creature-to-creature communication!

ANIMAL TALKS TO HUMAN

Meet Kanzi. Kanzi has about the same speech level as a human toddler. But this clever chatterbox is no human. He's a **bonobo,** a cousin of the chimpanzee.

When Kanzi was a baby, he used to go with his mom, Matata, to her language lessons at Georgia State University, in Atlanta, Georgia, U.S.A. Matata wasn't a very good student ... but little Kanzi was. One day when Matata was away, Kanzi surprised the scientists by using language they had been trying to teach his mom.

Kanzi talks by using a special board with symbols on it. The symbols represent different words, including "tickle" and "yogurt." He points at the symbols to communicate.

One time while out in the woods, Kanzi pointed to the symbols for "marshmallows" and "fire." A human handed him marshmallows and matches. He gathered twigs, carefully built them into a pile, lit them with the matches, and then toasted the marshmallows on a stick. Even apes can't resist s'mores!

Another time, a human showed Kanzi some yogurt. Kanzi made a noise. His sister Panbanisha heard Kanzi from the next room. She pointed to the symbol for "yogurt" on her board. That means that Kanzi's noise might have been a word for "yogurt" that his sister could understand. Maybe she wanted some, too!

Today, Kanzi knows the meaning of about 3,000 words. Talk about a grammar guru!

VS.

HUMAN TALKS TO ANIMAL

Denise Herzing sees a pod of Atlantic spotted dolphins and slips off her boat into the blue ocean water. The curious creatures swim right up to her. She's been studying the dolphins in this part of the Bahamas for nearly 30 years.

Herzing splashes and flips in the water, dolphins all around her. She and another researcher play keep-away with the dolphins using a piece of sargassum, a type of seaweed. Herzing wears a device strapped across her chest. It's a new invention that converts dolphin whistles into human language: a dolphin translator.

It's loud underwater. Dolphins whistle, click, and chatter. Scientists think they use these sounds to communicate. Herzing and her fellow researcher pass the sargassum back and forth as the dolphins watch. Herzing then presses a button, and the device she's wearing makes a whistling noise. Herzing's team is trying to teach the dolphins that the noise means "sargassum." She hopes that if the dolphins want a turn with the seaweed, they will repeat the whistle. Then the device will translate the whistle into English so Herzing can understand it.

Herzing and her team repeated this exercise many, many times. Then one day, it finally happened: In August 2013, Herzing was swimming with the dolphins when one of them whistled. The device on her chest spoke. It said, "sargassum." For the first time ever, Herzing's device had translated a dolphin whistle in real time.

There's a chance that the event might have been a coincidence—the dolphin whistle could just have sounded like the signal for seaweed by chance. But if the dolphin did it on purpose, Herzing could be close to learning whether dolphins truly have their own language. And, if they do, she might be on her way to finding out what they're talking about.

Tongue all twisted? Ha! Better get gabbing. It's time for some language puzzles!

Sounds Like a Winner

Circle your answers to the questions below. Then follow the directions after each question to learn a fun fact about language.

WHICH IS THE SMALLEST U.S. COIN, A SCENT OR A CENT?
If you chose "scent," put "warthogs" in box 1.
If you chose "cent," put "words" in box 1.

WHAT DO YOU CALL A SLICE OF A PIE, A PIECE OR A PEACE?
If you chose "piece," put "pronunciation" in box 2.
If you chose "peace," put "color" in box 2.

TO MOVE WATER, DO YOU POOR IT OR POUR IT?
If you chose "poor," put "moods" in box 3.
If you chose "pour," put "meanings" in box 3.

WHICH IS AN ANIMAL WITH ANTLERS, A DEAR OR A DEER?
If you chose "dear," put "hats" in box 4.
If you chose "deer," put "homonyms" in box 4.

words	THAT HAVE THE SAME	pronuction	BUT DIFFERENT	meanings	ARE	hs
1		2		3		4

Sign of the Times

Sign language is a way of communicating using hand signals.
American Sign Language (ASL) is the primary language of many deaf North Americans.

Though signs cover everything from "mother" to "thanks," ASL uses a manual alphabet
(or fingerspelling) for spelling names, places, titles, and other words that don't yet have signs.
Use the ASL alphabet below to decipher the name of the person who brought
sign language to the United States in 1817.

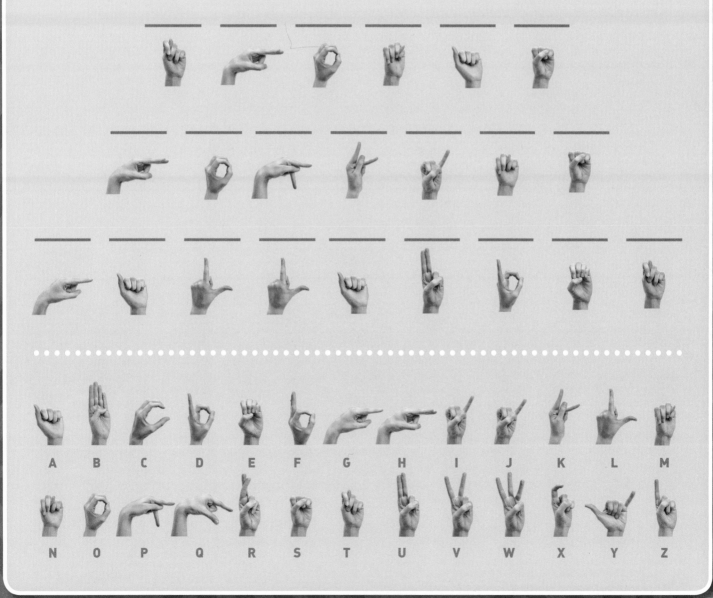

The Man Who Knew 50 Languages

IT TAKES MOST KIDS ABOUT THREE TO FIVE YEARS TO MASTER A NEW LANGUAGE. But for Ken Hale, 10 to 15 minutes was enough time to get the basics. Hale was a language expert who studied at the Massachusetts Institute of Technology in Cambridge, Massachusetts, U.S.A. By the time of his death in 2001, Hale knew about 50 languages. Most Americans know only one.

Hale's talent for languages amazed the people around him. He learned Jemez and Hopi, two Native American languages, from his roommates. He picked up the basics of Japanese after watching a Japanese film with subtitles. Friends saw him study Finnish on an airplane and start speaking it when the plane landed.

Hale's specialty was endangered languages. Languages become extinct when there are only a few people left who speak them. When those people die, their language dies with them. The language spoken by the Native American tribe that greeted the Pilgrims in 1620, Wampanoag, had no living speakers left by the middle of the 19th century. Hale helped revive this language, and now several thousand people around Cape Cod speak it. Hale thought each language was a work of art that deserved to be preserved. What a likeable linguist!

MYTHS

BUSTED!

MYTH: Albert Einstein failed math as a student.

BUSTED!: Einstein excelled at math from a young age.

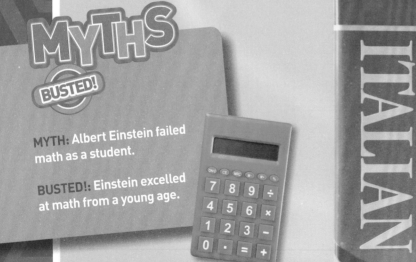

Untranslatables

Do you ever have the feeling that you can't find the word to express something? If you spoke as many languages as Ken Hale did, you might not have this problem. Check out these words from other cultures that have no English equivalent.

- *Waldeinsamkeit* (German): the feeling of being alone in the woods
- *Culaccino* (Italian): the mark a cold glass leaves on a table
- *Iktsuarpok* (Inuit): the frustration of waiting for someone to show up
- *Friolero* (Spanish): a person who is supersensitive to the cold
- *Age-otori* (Japanese): to look worse after a haircut
- *Pochemuchka* (Russian): a person who asks a lot of questions
- *Pana po'o* (Hawaiian): scratching your head to remember something you have forgotten

Ready for another cranial challenge? Try *this* talk test.

Ironic Fear

Though almost everyone is afraid of something, you may find this fear rather unusual. Someone with this fear would be afraid to write it down or tell you its name! Can you guess what the fear is?

Put ALL of these clues together for the answer.

+ +O+ -ER+ +QUIP+ +IO+FO+ +A

ANSWER

GENIUS GENUS:
CREATIVITY CHAMPION

Okay, if you didn't figure out this puzzle, you're not alone! The most important clue was when I told you to put ALL of the clues TOGETHER. See the solution and you'll understand why!

Pesky Palindromes

A palindrome is a word or phrase (or name!) that is the same when read forward and backward. The most famous palindrome is "ABLE WAS I ERE I SAW ELBA."

The trick to writing a palindrome is starting small.

Turn each of the partial words at right into a palindrome by using the same letter at the beginning and end of the word. We've completed the first one for you.

N OO N

_ EVE _

_ ADA _

_ OTO _

_ OLO _

_ AYA _

_ ANNA _

_ ACECA _

Auto Incorrect

My great-aunt Rebel finally bought a smart phone, but she isn't checking her texts before hitting "send." Autocorrect changed many of her words, and I have no clue what she's saying. If you can figure it out, let me know by correcting the words for me!

I was searching for Rezzi bees online, hoping to make some tasty Sam witches. Can you make some colds law? We need enough for for D people. You should ulcer bring that cough fee I scream from your flees' hair. This is going to be a blossom picnic! I might even try dumping soap with the squids this year!

Love,
You're on Tea Rebel

Flick of the Wrist

With the flick of my wrist I can change the meaning of any word! How do I do it? Easy, I use my pen to cross out a single letter! Let's see if you can do the same. Remove one letter from each word at right to create a word with an entirely new meaning. There is more than one answer for many of these!

BLACK - ___ = _____

NEAT - ___ = _____

WINDOW - ___ = _____

GOAT - ___ = _____

POUT - ___ = _____

PAIN - ___ = _____

GRAVE - ___ = _____

DIME - ___ = _____

Will It Fit?

A person with hippopotomonstrosesquippedaliophobia (fear of long words) may not want to live in a city and state like Minneapolis, Minnesota, which is 20 letters long. But believe it or not, there are even longer combinations, including Friendly Village of Crooked Creek, Georgia (36 letters), and Slovenska Narodna Podporna Jednota, Pennsylvania (43 letters). Personally, I think the shorter the better. I'd rather live in a place like Oz, Kentucky, where I could maybe find a wizard to help me with some of my formulas!

Where is one of the longest place names in the world?

Hint: A=1, Z=26

D	A	N	G	O	C	
2	1	14	7	11	15	11

20	8	1	9	12	1	14	4

GENIUS GENUS:
LOGICAL LEADER

Road Trip

Gamma Rae has been on the telephone all day making reservations for a whirlwind vacation across the U.S. Unfortunately, Gamma sometimes gets letters mixed up when she's writing, so we're not exactly sure what she's planning. Can you unscramble the city names at right help us figure out where Gamma's going?

(Hint: Some of these cities are two words.)

1. **LETS EAT, Washington** _Seattle_
2. **BOIL ME RAT, Maryland** _____
3. **LOB MUCUS, Ohio** _____
4. **I WAKE MULE, Wisconsin** _____
5. **NOSH OUT, Texas** _____
6. **ASK ICY ANTS, Kansas** _____
7. **ENSNARE OWL, Louisiana** _____
8. **I SPIN A LEMON, Minnesota** _____
9. **SNAP A LION, Maryland** _____
10. **SKIM CRAB, North Dakota** _____
11. **TEAM CAR SON, California** _____

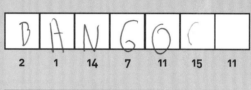

No Rhyme This Time

I won't say a word
About what I've heard
As this is the time
To talk about "rhyme."
A type of speech
Within your reach,
Only through sound
Will rhymes be found!

GENIUS GENUS:
WORD WIZARD

All right, my little geniuses, now that you know what a rhyme is, I'm challenging you to find eight words that have no rhyme in English. Use the hints below if you must! Then, test your answers by trying to find their rhymes (using the sound and not the spelling of the words).

If you find a rhyme, then you haven't found the answer!

1. _____ (Plant one for a tulip to bloom)

2. _____ (Popular citrus)

3. _____ (Type of fish, or spiritual messenger)

4. _____ (Metal used in jewelry and utensils)

5. _____ (12 of these in a year)

6. _____ (Not true)

7. _____ (Large-tusked marine mammal)

8. _____ (Insect with quite a sting)

GOOD vs. EVIL
Superbrain
Showdown

WELL, WELL, WELL. LOOKS LIKE YOU SMOOTH-TALKED YOUR WAY TO THE END OF THIS CHAPTER. But what happens when you have to go head-to-head with a true genius of gab? See if you can get these four questions right. G.O.O.D. needs all the help it can get!

1. The Zuni have a hard time telling the colors orange and yellow apart. This may be because ...

11. their eyesight is weak.

13. they don't learn their colors when they are young.

12. their language doesn't have separate words for orange and yellow.

20. they wear sunglasses all the time.

2. How does Kanzi communicate with humans?

5.	He points to symbols on a board that represent words.
17.	He uses sign language.
10.	He draws what he is trying to say.
13.	He recites Shakespeare plays.

MASTERMIND METER

YOU ARE HERE

70% COMPLETE

3. What is the function of the special device Denise Herzing wears?

19.	It keeps her afloat.
5.	It holds treats for the dolphins she studies.
18.	It records dolphin movements.
20.	It translates dolphin whistles into English words.

4. It takes the average child three to five years to master a language. How long did it take Ken Hale?

| 20. | 10–15 minutes | 8. | one year |
| 9. | one month | 11. | one decade |

RECORD YOUR ANSWERS HERE

1	2	3	4
10			

CHAPTER EIGHT

While You're Sleeping

Feeling pretty confident in your cranium?
Well, then, riddle me this, Mastermind:

Every creature on the planet does it—from the teensiest gnat to the biggest blue whale. Even you do it. In fact, you spend a third of your life doing it. What is it?

Did you guess? Or was that a little too tricky for your meager mind? The answer is sleep. If you live to age 90, you will have spent 32 years snoozing. That's a big chunk of your life! So, sleep must be important. Ready for the really weird part, though? Experts aren't sure why we do it.

Sleep is one of the science's biggest mysteries. To find out more, read on. Just don't nod off, or you'll miss something.

Trace all the lines inside the brain without ever lifting your pencil and without tracing the same line twice.

Slumber Secrets

WHEN YOU FALL ASLEEP, IT FEELS LIKE YOUR BRAIN IS SHUTTING DOWN. Sleep can seem like a big waste of time, right? Amazingly, however, some areas of your brain are actually *more* active while you're asleep than they are while you're awake. You're snoozing away, but your noggin is hard at work! Here's what it's up to after you doze off.

SLEEP COASTER

Sleep may feel calm, but it's actually kind of like a roller coaster ride for your brain! Once you hit the pillow, your brain goes through five different stages of sleep. Each one is a little different, and you cycle through them all about five times every night. What a wild ride!

Stage 3
In this medium sleep stage, if someone whispered to you, you probably wouldn't hear them. Your tissues, skin, and hair grow and repair themselves—much faster than they do at any time when you're awake.

Stage 2
You're in light sleep. Your heart rate slows, and your body temperature begins to drop.

Stage 1
Here, at the top of the roller coaster ride, is when you begin to drift away from the world around you.

NORMAL SLEEP PATTERN

Scientists think that sleep, especially in the REM stage, is very important for keeping your mind and body healthy. Here's a little of what they've found out so far. It may surprise you!

MEMORY MACHINE

Having trouble remembering the formula to find the area of a circle? Try going to bed. Your brain will work on the problem while you're asleep!

While you're snoozing, your brain is also busy strengthening memories. Matthew Walker, a sleep scientist at the University of California, Berkeley, conducted a study in which he asked his subjects to memorize a sequence of numbers. He had some people learn the sequence in the morning and then tested their memory. He tested them again before they went to bed that night. Walker found that they remembered the sequence about as well at night as they had in the morning.

Walker asked other study subjects to learn the sequence late in the day, then tested them. Just as he did for the first group, Walker gave them a second test later. But this time, he waited until the next morning, after they'd had gotten a full night's sleep. He found that, overnight, they'd gotten 30 percent better at the task. His conclusion? Sleep made their memories stronger!

CREATIVE CRANIUM

Want to come up with the next great invention, like a robot that does your homework for you? Make sure to get some rest. A good snooze could lead to your million-dollar idea!

Another study by sleep scientist Matthew Walker found that sleep helps your brain make connections between unrelated thoughts. Those connections lead to those "aha!" moments when creative ideas are born. His study found that people were 33 percent more likely to make creative connections after some solid sack time. That's my kind of brainpower!

Stage 5

After about an hour asleep, your brain starts to climb back up the stages toward waking. It chugs up from Stage 4, to 3, to 2. But, before you hit Stage 1 and start to wake up, your brain does something very strange: It enters Stage 5, **REM (Rapid Eye Movement) sleep.** REM sleep is when you dream.

During this sleep stage, your brain becomes very active, and some parts of your body begin to wake up. Your eyes start to move around under your eyelids (giving Rapid Eye Movement sleep its name).

Stage 4

This is the deepest kind of sleep. It's very difficult for someone to wake you up in stage four sleep. Your body continues to repair itself during this stage.

90 MINUTES

Wake up, Mastermind!
Get your brain moving, because
it's time for more Time Trials.

Two letters have been swapped throughout this puzzle (but not necessarily the same two letters as in the last chapters!)
Unswap the letters to reveal the hidden message.

LETTER SWAP

S	E	A	H	T	T	E	R	S	O	H	L	D
O	A	N	D	S	W	O	E	N	T	O	E	Y
S	L	E	E	P	T	H	P	R	E	V	E	N
T	D	R	I	F	T	I	N	G	A	W	A	Y
F	R	H	M	H	N	E	A	N	H	T	O	E
R

___ _____ ____ _____ _____ _____

_____ __ _____ _____ ____

_____ ___ _____.

**TOTAL TIME TO
COMPLETE PUZZLE**

See the hint at the bottom of the page if you need help discovering the hidden expression in this rebus!

REBUS

DREAMS

HINT: What is happening to the word?

ANSWER

TOTAL TIME TO
COMPLETE PUZZLE

Creature Sleepers

WHEN I NEED A NAP, I JUST CURL UP ON MY DOG BED IN THE LAB. But for the rest of the animal kingdom, catching some z's isn't always so easy. Some sleeping animals risk life and limb just to get some shut-eye. Here are four creatures that don't let the wild get in the way of their naptimes.

WATER BED

Dolphins live underwater, but they breathe air. If they zonked out like you do, they would drown while they were dozing. So how do dolphins sleep?

When a dolphin snoozes, it rests only half of its brain at a time. It closes one eye, and the opposite side of its brain shuts down. This is called **unihemispheric sleep.** Over the course of the day, each half of the dolphin's brain gets about four hours of deep sleep. The "awake" half stays active to let the dolphin know when it's time to come up for air.

This method of sleeping not only keeps dolphins from drowning but also lets them keep one eye out for hungry predators at all times. What a smart slumber strategy!

FEATHERED FRAUD

Male malachite sunbirds have bright yellow tufts of feathers on their chests. For a long time, scientists didn't know what the sunbirds used these feathers for. After researchers used infrared cameras to watch the birds after dark, they saw that the sunbirds puff up their chest tufts when they fall asleep. Conclusion? The puffed tufts may ward off predators. A creature on the hunt for a feathered feast might look at the sunbird's bright tufts and think it's staring into the yellow eyes of a big, scary beast. It's nature's "Do Not Disturb" sign!

ROCK-A-BYE APE-Y

Most wild creatures don't have a soft bed to snuggle up in at the end of a long day. Many species of monkeys, such as baboons, spend the night sitting upright in trees far above the ground, trying not to doze off so they don't take a nighttime nosedive. **Orangutans** sleep in trees, too. But that doesn't stop them from getting comfy at night.

These **apes,** along with others in their family—gorillas, chimps, and bonobos—build nests in the treetops to sleep in. To create these leafy beds, they break branches and weave them together. But it's not as easy as it might sound. It takes a long time to become a master nestbuilder. Orangutans begin practicing when they're six months old, and it takes them until age three or four to do it well. What a nifty sleep skill!

LEND A PAW

Sea otters drift off to dreamland while floating on their backs in the sea. But they have to be careful not to drift away, or they might wake up far away from home. So when it's time for a snooze, the savvy otters sometimes wrap themselves in seaweed. This keeps them anchored in place.

Sea otters have been spotted snoozing away in groups of up to 100—all securely wrapped up in their seaweed anchors. And that's not sea otters' only strategy for staying together while they sleep—sometimes, they'll hold paws. Say it with me now: *Awww!*

Jokes

I'll tell you a joke or two that always makes Atom ROFL (roll on the floor, laughing), which isn't that hard for a dog.

Let's see which of you creative geniuses out there can figure out the answers:

1. What do trees do to get some sleep?

2. Where do tree snakes love to go to sleep?

Catch Some Z's

Cartoon artists often use the letter Z to indicate sleep.

How many Z's can you find in the image at right ?

Is that a yawn I see? Better take a power nap, Mastermind. You'll need to be sharp to tackle these puzzles!

GENIUS GENUS: SPATIAL SUPERSTAR

Doggie Dreams

Scientists believe dogs dream. I wonder what they dream about? Spot the 13 differences between these two pictures that imagine what canines may see when they slumber.

The Man Who Didn't Sleep

WHAT HAPPENS WHEN YOU STOP SLEEPING? Scientists have a pretty good idea, thanks in part to a radio DJ named Peter Tripp. On January 21, 1959, Tripp decided to stay awake on air for at least 200 hours—more than eight days. His "wake-a-thon" would raise money for charity.

For the first few days of his sleep stunt, Tripp stayed awake without too much trouble. But after 100 hours of no shut-eye, things started to get interesting. Tripp could no longer solve simple math problems or recite the alphabet. And after 120 hours, he started to **hallucinate,** or see things that weren't there.

Tripp thought he saw mice and kittens running around the radio studio. He was sure his shoes were full of spiders. He opened a desk drawer and saw a fire that wasn't there. When a doctor came to examine him toward the end of his no-nap feat, Tripp thought the man was an undertaker come to bury him. Terrified, Tripp ran into the street. Not sleeping was driving Tripp crazy!

Tripp nods off during his stay-awake marathon.

What was happening inside Tripp's brain? His noggin was desperate for REM sleep, but Tripp wouldn't let himself nod off. So his brain decided to go into REM sleep anyway. Tripp was dreaming while he was still awake! Though his dreams were scary, they were totally normal—he just wasn't having them in bed.

After 201 hours and 10 minutes, Tripp called it quits. He went to bed and slept for 13 hours. When he woke up, he felt fine. Despite his nightmare of a wake-a-thon, his brain was able to reset itself back to normal after clocking a sleep session. But I bet he thought twice about trying the sleep stunt again!

Can Not Sleeping Kill You?

As the story of Peter Tripp shows, not getting enough sleep isn't good for you. But can you actually die from lack of sleep?

In 1836, a 45-year-old Italian man named Giacomo fell ill with a mysterious sickness that left him unable to sleep. He lay in bed, exhausted, but no matter how he tried, he couldn't nod off. Giacomo grew more and more delirious, and, eventually, he died. The priests who took care of him noted his cause of death as dementia. But the real killer was a disease that hadn't yet been identified: **fatal familial insomnia,** or **FFI.**

Giacomo's descendants grew up to be successful doctors and businesspeople. But like Giacomo, many of them were stricken with a strange illness in middle age. Sufferers who inherit the disease spend most of their lives healthy. But then, in their early 50s, they suddenly find themselves unable to sleep through the night. No matter what they try, they can't drift off. Their bodies start to show signs of distress: high blood pressure, rapid pulse, and heavy sweating. After months of sleeplessness, they begin to grow delirious. They lose their ability to walk and speak. Eventually, they die.

But don't worry, Mastermind—FFI is incredibly rare. It has been found in just 40 families worldwide. So if you find yourself tossing and turning, don't panic. A sleepless night or two won't harm you.

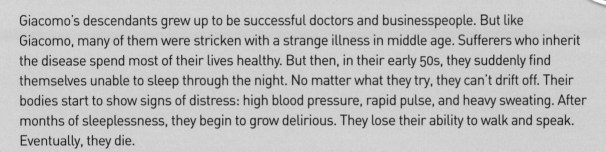

IMA GENIUS'S BRAINIAC BONUS: COUNT TO 12

Want a hint, brainiac? Sometimes we get the right answer only after we put the pieces together!

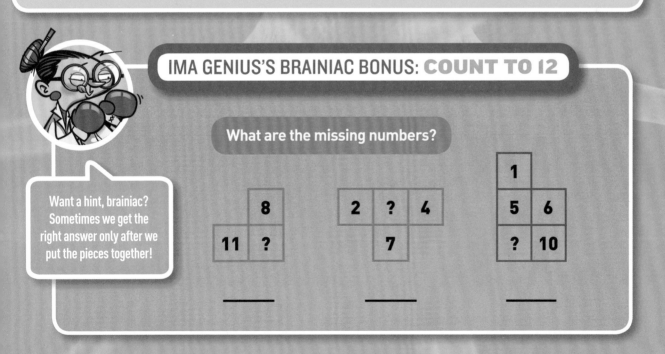

What are the missing numbers?

	8
11	?

____

2	?	4
	7	

____

1	
5	6
?	10

____

I hope you got your rest last night, Mastermind. Only a nimble noggin will be able to solve these mindbenders!

Color That Dream

In dreams, sometimes we have to fill in missing information to understand the full story.

Can you add the missing vowels (A, E, I, O, U) to figure out what is being said below?

Hint: There are two sentences that end with the same word.

Sleeping Animals

Most animals sleep a consistent number of hours each day (or night).

Use the hidden hints below to discover which animal sleeps an average of only 1.9 hours each day.

DOG
(10.6 hours)

TIGER
(15.8 hours)

SQUIRREL
(14.9 hours)

CAT
(12.1 hours)

FERRET
(14.5 hours)

FISH
(Guppy, 7 hours)

MOUSE
(12.1 hours)

(1.9 hours)

MYTHS BUSTED!

MYTH: Naps are a waste of time.

BUSTED!: Short naps can boost alertness, mood, and memory. Many famous thinkers in history were nappers, such as physicist Albert Einstein and political leader Winston Churchill.

Atom and I were recently discussing the sleep habits of some creatures. Here's the conversation we had:

IMA: I once knew a guy who slept upside down.
ATOM: Really? What's his name?
IMA: Dracula.
ATOM: Yeah, he's kind of batty.

Ready for another challenge? These puzzles are so tricky they'll make your eyeballs fall right out of your skull! Just kidding—that probably won't happen.

Bedtime Wish

Hopefully you got enough sleep last night to allow your creative side help you with this puzzle.

What is a common phrase often heard at bedtime?

GENIUS GENUS: CREATIVITY CHAMPION

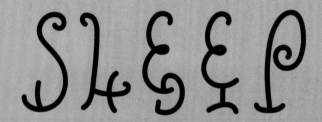

Are you stuck? Then read on ...

If you think the answer is "SLEEP," you have half of the answer. Turn the book upside down to finish this bedtime wish.

Dreams

There are many types of puzzles (and dreams!), and we've listed three at right. You'll need to unscramble, show your superior rebus skills, and engage in some letter play.

Hint: The animal in puzzle 2 is an adult female!

1 **READ MY ADS**

2  +

3 Letter that **s**ometimes has **s**ame **s**ound as C + A pronoun that describes you and another person + E + Cozy letter never found in coffee = **DREAMS**

The Framework of Sleep

Complete the puzzle from the word list below.
Hint: Start with the longest word first!

GENIUS GENUS:
WORD WIZARD

3 LETTERS
BED
DAY
REM

4 LETTERS
IDEA
NEST

5 LETTERS
AWAKE
BRAIN
DREAM
NIGHT

6 LETTERS
HEALTH
MEMORY
REPAIR
STAGES

7 LETTERS
PATTERN
PROBLEM

8 LETTERS
CREATIVE
POWER NAP

9 LETTERS
DEEP SLEEP
NIGHTMARE

11 LETTERS
HALLUCINATE

GOOD vs. EVIL
Superbrain Showdown

OK, MASTERMIND, I'M RESTED AND READY TO TAKE YOU ON IN ANOTHER SUPERBRAIN SHOWDOWN.
My memories are mastered and my creativity channeled. You're going to need all your brainpower to beat me this time! See if you can get all these questions right and defeat me at my genius game.

1. Which of the following is NOT true about REM sleep?

6. It stands for Rapid Eye Movement sleep.

16. It's the sleep stage when dreams occur.

23. During REM sleep, your body is paralyzed.

5. Your brain is inactive during REM sleep.

MASTERMIND METER

2. Dolphins rest one half of their brain at a time. What is this called?

18. **Unihemispheric sleep**
25. **Unilateral sleep**
14. **Stage 4 sleep**
11. **Divided**

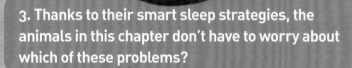

3. Thanks to their smart sleep strategies, the animals in this chapter don't have to worry about which of these problems?

17. **Being eaten by predators while snoozing**
22. **Drowning while sleeping**
16. **Drifting away from their family while dozing**
19. **all of the above**

YOU ARE HERE

80% COMPLETE

4. After 120 hours of sleep deprivation, Peter Tripp started to hallucinate. What does that mean?

23. **He nodded off uncontrollably.**
2. **He saw things that weren't there.**
5. **He told stories that didn't make sense.**
15. **He stopped talking.**

RECORD YOUR ANSWERS HERE

1	2	3	4
5	18	22	2

CHAPTER NINE

Mind Control

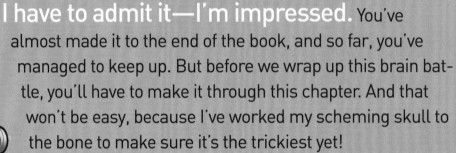

I have to admit it—I'm impressed. You've almost made it to the end of the book, and so far, you've managed to keep up. But before we wrap up this brain battle, you'll have to make it through this chapter. And that won't be easy, because I've worked my scheming skull to the bone to make sure it's the trickiest yet!

You might be wondering what I plan to do if I defeat you in this cranial challenge. Why, I'm going to take over your brain, of course! Then I'm going to force you to use your noggin for E.V.I.L. instead of G.O.O.D.

What's that, you say? You think that kind of mental takeover is impossible? Ha! You're such an innocent intellectual. Turn the page to learn about the science of brain domination ... unless you're too scared!

Trace all the lines inside the brain without ever lifting your pencil and without tracing the same line twice.

Intelligence Invasion

IS IT POSSIBLE TO GET INSIDE SOMEONE'S BRAIN?

Read about these brain-control experiments and make up your own mind.

MIND MELD

Imagine if an evil genius like me could connect my brain to someone else's. I could make someone carry out my nefarious deeds from afar! It sounds like science fiction, but this technology might be closer than you think.

Scientists placed a pair of rats in a chamber with two levers. Above each lever was a light. When one of the lights switched on, the rats learned to press the lever below it to get a treat. After the rats mastered this mission, the researchers put the rats in separate chambers and used a very thin wire to connect their brains. When the scientists lit up one of the lights in Rat A's cage, Rat A pressed the correct lever and got a treat. No light went on in Rat B's cage, but it, too, pressed the correct lever and got a treat!

When Rat A pressed the lever, its brain signals passed through the wire to Rat B. Rat B could get the information directly from Rat A's mind. The researchers repeated the experiment over and over. Rat B chose the correct lever 70 percent of the time. Some scientists think that someday this technology could be used to share information directly between human brains. What do you think—is that cool or just plain creepy?

SKATEBOARD OF THE FUTURE

In 2013, a company called Chaotic Moon Labs showed off a new skateboard at a technology convention. It's motorized, has chunky all-terrain tires, weighs 100 pounds (45 kg) ... and can be controlled by a human mind!

This invention, called the Board of Imagination, comes with a headset that reads the rider's brainwaves. You simply climb aboard and think about where you want to go, and the Board of Imagination takes you there. You'd better be a good mental driver, though, because the board tops out at a speedy 32 miles an hour (52 km/h)!

This design is just a prototype, but someday a skateboard like this could be your new ride to school. That would be quite a cranial commute!

MIND READER

Soldiers scan the landscape in front of their convoy of military vehicles. They're looking for signs of a hidden bomb, like a flash of metal or freshly moved soil. How fast they can react to these slight signals can mean the difference between life and death.

Experienced soldiers are very good at spotting bomb threats. The problem, as you learned in chapter 4, is that the unconscious mind can detect something before the conscious mind is even aware of it. So even though the soldiers' brains have a built-in threat detector, it might not immediately alert them to sound the alarm.

Scientists at the Defense Advanced Research Projects Agency (DARPA)—a U.S. government agency that develops military technology—are working on a way to harness that unconscious ability. Their new device is called the Cognitive Technology Threat Warning System. Here's how it works. A special pair of goggles flashes images of the landscape to the wearer's eyes—about 10 images per second. A headset monitors brain activity. When the brain spots something that might be a bomb, it gives off a certain signal, called the P-300 brainwave. The headset senses this signal and alerts the wearer that his brain has detected danger. In tests, this device helped the wearers spot 30 percent more threats.

BYE-BYE BRAIN

What makes you grab a product off the store shelf and decide to buy it? Research shows that people can't always express why they make certain purchasing choices. A new field of brain science called **neuromarketing** looks directly inside shoppers' brains to find out why they make their buying decisions.

What is it about Cheetos—the best-selling brand of cheese puffs in in the United States—that people like so much? In 2008, the Frito-Lay company wanted to know. So the company hired neuromarketing experts to figure it out. The experts scanned the brains of Cheetos-eaters and found that snackers' brains were strongly responding to something a little odd. It wasn't the Cheetos' taste or texture that made their brains light up. It was the sticky, orange stuff that coated their fingers as they ate the salty treat. Their brains were getting a secret kick from the Cheetos mess!

Frito-Lay used this information to create a new marketing campaign. The company released commercials that showed off the orange dust in the hope of selling more Cheetos. So the next time a commercial gives you a hankering, you should wonder—what is it doing to manipulate your craving?

TiME TRiALS

I hope you're feeling sharp, Mastermind. It's our last Time Trials, and I'm pulling out all the stops. Can you solve each of these in under two minutes and put me to shame?

Two letters have been swapped throughout this puzzle (but not necessarily the same two letters as in the last chapters!). Unswap the letters to reveal the hidden message.

LETTER **SWAP**

P	A	T	R	E	N	T	S	C	A	N	B	E	A
W	A	K	E	D	U	I	R	N	G	B	I	A	R
N	S	U	I	G	E	I	Y	B	E	C	A	U	S
E	T	H	E	I	E	A	I	E	N	O	P	A	R
N	I	E	C	E	P	T	O	I	S	R	N	T	H
E	B	I	A	R	N								

_____ ___ ___ ___ ___

_____ _____ ____ _____

____ _____ ___ __ ___

_ _____ __ ___ _____.

TOTAL TIME TO COMPLETE PUZZLE

| | | : | | |

See the hint at the bottom of the page if you need help discovering the hidden expression in this rebus!

REBUS

TH

HINT: Where are the letters "TH"?

ANSWER

TOTAL TIME TO COMPLETE PUZZLE

E.V.I.L. Masterminds of the Animal Kingdom

YOU THINK ALL US ANIMALS ARE JUST CUTE AND FUZZY, HUH? Silly human. The critters on these pages will stop at nothing to take over other brains. What beastly beasts!

CRAZY CAT

Imagine if you felt no fear. On the one hand, you could watch scary movies without having nightmares afterward. Fun! But on the other hand, you might walk into a busy street in front of a moving car. Not fun!

That might sound far-fetched, but it's exactly what happens to rodents infected with a mind-controlling parasite called *Toxoplasma gondii*. When this tiny organism infects a mouse, it heads straight to the brain and takes control to make the infected rodent lose its natural fear of cats. A mouse that stops hiding from a predator when it smells one coming becomes an easy target. What a devious disease!

T. gondii doesn't just infect rats and mice. As many as half the world's human population is infected, too. For a long time, scientists thought *T. gondii* just gave humans mild flu-like symptoms. But now, some scientists think it could also be changing human behavior, just like it changes the behavior of rodents. In some cases, this tiny terror could affect how much you trust others, how you deal with scary situations, and even which smells you like. Spooky!

SPIDER SLAVES

When the wasp *Hymenoepimecis argyraphaga* is ready to give birth, it looks for a spider. It crawls onto the spider's belly and lays a tiny egg there. Later, a little wormlike **larva**—a baby wasp—crawls out of the egg. The larva makes small holes in the spider's skin and sucks out the spider's fluids through the holes. The larva grows bigger and stronger as it feasts on the spider's insides. While it feeds, the larva also secretes a chemical into the spider that changes how the spider behaves. The spider stops spinning its normal symmetrical web. Its new web is stronger and has a new shape: It's just right to hold the growing larva.

After about a week, the spider is just a shriveled shell. The larva attaches itself to the new web and creates a cocoon. Protected there in the web made by its spider slave, the larva safely grows into a new wasp.

ZOMBIE ANTS

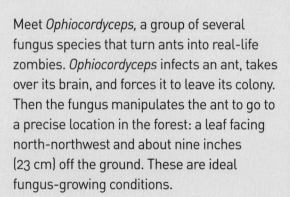

Zombies are terrifying monsters that will stop at nothing to bite their next victim. But zombies exist only in scary books and movies ... right?

Meet *Ophiocordyceps,* a group of several fungus species that turn ants into real-life zombies. *Ophiocordyceps* infects an ant, takes over its brain, and forces it to leave its colony. Then the fungus manipulates the ant to go to a precise location in the forest: a leaf facing north-northwest and about nine inches (23 cm) off the ground. These are ideal fungus-growing conditions.

Compelled by the fungus that now rules its brain, the ant bites into the underside of the leaf. It dies. Then something even stranger happens. A stalk grows out the back of the ant's head. This horrible hat rains **spores**— baby fungi—down onto other still-healthy ants below. The zombie fungus attaches to its new victims, and the brain takeover starts again. Yikes!

PEST CONTROL

Wasps must be especially wicked. Another species, called the **jewel wasp,** also takes over another insect's brain to raise its children. Female jewel wasps use cockroaches as living nurseries.

First, the jewel wasp stings the roach and injects it with venom. The venom targets the part of the roach's brain that controls movement. The roach is still able to move, but it no longer has the free will to decide when and where to go.

The jewel wasp grabs the roach by its antenna. Like a human walking a dog, the wasp guides the helpless roach into a burrow. There, she lays her eggs on its body. When the wasp larvae are born, the roach becomes their first meal.

Still shaking in your boots from the evil animals on the last page? Snap out of it, Mastermind—you'll need your wits about you to solve these puzzles.

Deal of the Day

Those neuromarketers may be clever, but I'm betting they're not as smart as my geniuses in training! I bet you can spot a deal from a mile away!

Prove me right by circling the better deal for each of these products.

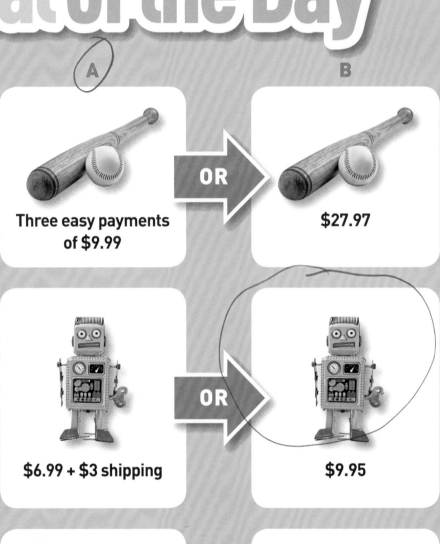

A   B

Three easy payments of $9.99   OR $27.97

$6.99 + $3 shipping   OR $9.95

$3.60 per dozen   OR $0.50 each

Zombie Zigzag

The Zombie leader has given you a choice: Get turned into a zombie or give him what he really wants—cheese puffs. (He loves that sticky orange dust, and he just can't get it off his mind!) Make your way through the aisles of the grocery store to reach the puffs (orange circle) and then the exit or you will become a mindless Zombie!

Don't go through any red patches—they're "hot" zones, full of Zombies!

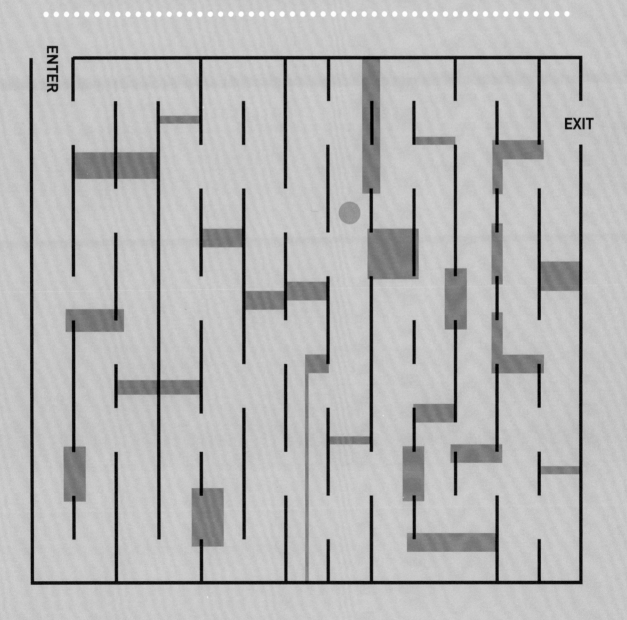

ENTER

EXIT

Flipping a Switch to Control the Brain

IN 2006, SCIENTISTS TURNED ON A TINY LASER. On one end, the laser was attached to a very thin cable; on the other, it was connected to the brain of a sleeping mouse, touching the part of the mouse's brain that controls waking. When the laser's light traveled down the cable and hit the mouse's brain, the mouse started to move. The flip of a switch made the mouse wake up on command.

Using light to manipulate the brain is called **optogenetics.** By targeting different brain areas, scientists can flip a switch to make mice run, lose their fear of open spaces, or choose one drink instead of another they normally prefer. Optogenetics is one of the fastest-growing fields in science.

It all started when a neuroscientist named Karl Deisseroth, from Stanford University in California, U.S.A., was studying algae. Inside a certain type of algae are molecules called **opsins.** Opsins can sense light—you have them, too, in your eyes. The algae use opsins to sense the direction of sunlight, which they use to create energy. What Deisseroth found most interesting was the fact that opsins are powered by electricity—just like the neurons in the brain. Could he use opsins to communicate with the brain?

Deisseroth and his team put opsin genes inside mouse neurons that control sleep and waking. That made those neurons sensitive to light. Then the researchers used a small laser to send a flash of light to those neurons. It worked. They could now wake up a mouse—or make it run, or turn left, or do just about any other behavior—just by flipping a light switch.

By making different neurons light-sensitive, flipping the switch, and watching what happens, scientists can see what behaviors the neurons

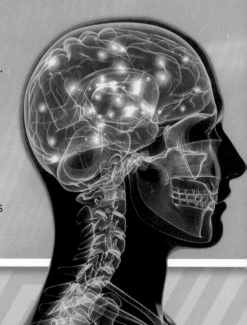

control. One set might make mice turn left; another might make them hungry. By working their way from one set of neurons to the next, researchers hope to use optogenetics to create the first ever map of all the brain's neurons and their functions.

Knowing the function of every neuron in the brain would be incredibly useful for scientists. For one thing, it could help treat human diseases. **Epilepsy,** for example, is a condition that makes certain neurons malfunction, causing a seizure—shaking of the muscles that can be dangerous. Optogenetics could target those faulty neurons and stop the seizures. Now that's using mind control for G.O.O.D.!

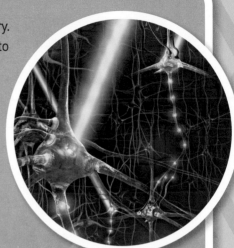

IMA GENIUS'S BRAINIAC BONUS: IT BOGGLES THE MIND

Connect letters in the grid at right to form words. You may change direction whenever you need, but once you draw a line through a letter, that letter cannot be used again for that word. (In other words, you can have more than one T in a word, as long as they are from different locations.)

To make this puzzle genius-worthy, find 11 words that are in this chapter (and I don't mean small, insignificant words like "IS" or "OR").

E	S	U	M	T
B	C	O	E	S
R	A	I	N	E
S	L	A	T	U
G	M	O	R	I
E	A	N	T	S

1. _____   7. _____

2. _____   8. _____

3. _____   9. _____

4. _____   10. _____

5. _____   11. _____

6. _____

You'd better try your hardest to solve these devious mental challenges. If you don't, your brain will be mine—all mine!

Sneaky Advertising

If you take a close look at these ads below, you'll see that the companies have hidden the names of some animals in their slogans. Are they giving you a subtle message about what you can expect from their services? You decide.

(example: "Author Seaside Retreat—no animals allowed" hides the word "horse" in "Author Seaside.")

GENIUS GENUS: CREATIVITY CHAMPION

Larry's Limousine Service
The limo used by cheese lovers.

Pandora Taxi Company
We're known for our cleanliness.

Salami Central
is rodent free.

Marve's Motel
Where a superhero achieves fame!

Wayne's Wrestling Ring
Hear the roar of sumo thunder.

Crazy Costumes
Wardrobe area is danger free.

24 HRS

Lunch!

Ima was supposed to meet me in the kitchen for lunch, but all I found was a mixed-up note she left on the fridge! Can you help me unscramble the words with red letters so I know what she's trying to tell me?

IBARN **TISSUE** ASH **A TEXTURE** HATT **IS VERY** MAILSIR **TO** FOUT.

GENIUS GENUS:
WORD WIZARD

BB9

Confusing Squares

Color the last row with the correct colors. Be careful! Your brain may try to trick you. Hint: Each color-shape combination has a match.

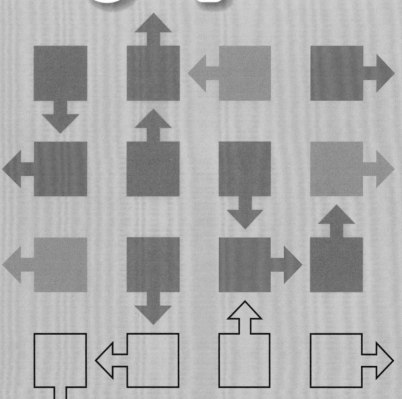

Buried in the Past

Ancient Egyptians used mummification to preserve bodies for the afterlife. The first step involved removing select internal organs and placing them in canopic jars. (Other organs ended up in the trash.)

Decode the labels below to discover where the various organs ended up.

Note: You'll need to really get creative here, Mastermind! As you can see below, some symbols correspond to more than one letter, so this won't be a perfect letter-by-letter translation. For example, I and E use the same symbol, as do U, V, and W.

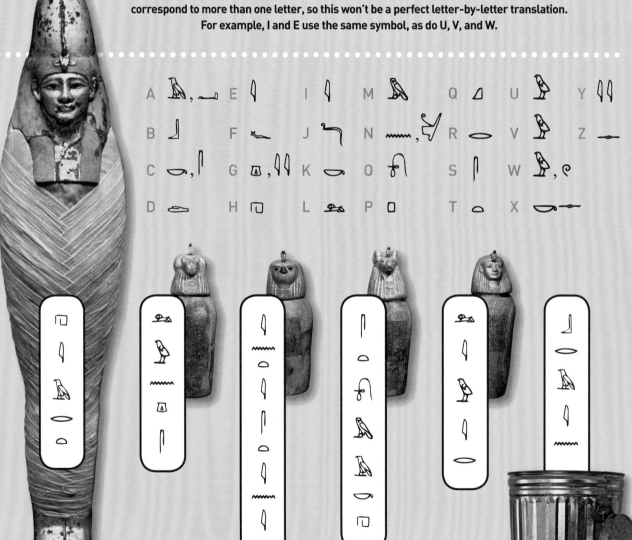

Unauthorized Experiment

GENIUS GENUS: LOGICAL LEADER

It's come to my attention that one or more of the geniuses who successfully completed the first Mastermind book (no, this is not my first time leading a bunch of bright kids through Genius Training) has been conducting an unauthorized experiment on me. On ME—of all people! This must stop now! The culprit(s) has been observing me and taking notes about everything I do, trying to influence me into making this book longer. Well, I will put a stop to this!

Whoever helps me figure out the culprit(s) behind this unauthorized experiment will graduate with top honors! Here's a list of suspects and my notes on the culprit(s):

TOP 10 SUSPECTS

NAME	AGE	STATE	FAVORITE SUBJECT
1. Abigail	10	ID	Spanish
2. Andrew	11	OH	Art
3. Jack	9	CA	History
4. Ben	13	GA	World Cultures
5. Chris	12	KS	Science
6. Emma	8	MN	Math
7. Ava	9	NY	English
8. Jack	7	SC	Math
9. Olivia	11	MI	Science
10. Daniel	9	PA	History

FACTS ABOUT THE CULPRIT(S)

- Comes from a state with six or more letters
- Favorite subject has seven letters
- Has at least two vowels in his/her name
- Name has at least one letter in common with his/her state

ANSWER

GOOD vs. EVIL
Superbrain Showdown

HERE WE ARE, THE FINAL SUPERBRAIN SHOWDOWN OF THE BOOK. If you don't mind my saying, I never thought you'd make it this far. But you're proving to be quite the cranial competitor.

So let's put your smarts to the test, shall we? You'll have to try your hardest to get all four of these questions right. May the better brain win!

1. Scientists have ...

24. connected the brains of two rats so that information could pass directly from one to the other.

21. used neuromarketing to figure out something people like about Cheetos that they didn't know themselves.

18. created a device that boosts soldiers' brains so they can detect threats faster.

5. all of the above

2. The parasitic organism *Toxoplasma gondii* grows in cats' bodies. What does it do when it infects a rat?

17. It makes the rat hide from its predators.

3. It makes the rat run more slowly.

12. It makes the rat lose its fear of cats.

7. It makes the rat crave cheese.

3. Which of the following is NOT something some wasps do?

25. inject a chemical into spiders' brains to make them spin a web to protect the wasp larva

13. use venom to paralyze cockroaches so the wasps can lead them wherever they want

15. control the behavior of butterflies so the wasps can ride them like hang gliders

18. take over other insects' brains to help them raise their young

4. What is optogenetics?

23. a new field of science that uses light to turn neurons on and off, controlling behavior

9. a technology that can be used to control the minds of anyone, anywhere

2. a super-advanced pair of eyeglasses

16. a field of science dreamed up by the neuroscientists of E.V.I.L.

MASTERMIND METER

YOU ARE HERE

90% COMPLETE

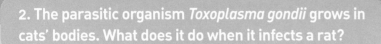

RECORD YOUR ANSWERS HERE

1 2 3 4

Battle of the Brainiacs

SO, YOU THOUGHT YOU WERE FINISHED? NO WAY! I've spent the entire book waiting for this moment. I've got you right where I want you, Mastermind. It's time for your brain to become mine!

When we first met, your noggin was nothing more than a puny pipsqueak. Why, I could have defeated you in my sleep! And it's too bad I didn't—you've done some brain bulking, Mastermind. Now you have a mighty mentality that nearly matches mine. (I won't say you're my egg-headed equal. That would be going too far.)

I'm the E.V.I.L. queen of mental manipulation. I've taken over multitudes of minds. And your impressive performance in this cranial competition has only made me want yours more. Your brain will be the crowning jewel of my collection.

I've got one more puzzle for you. If you can solve it, you'll escape my clutches. But this one is so wonderfully wicked, so deliciously devious, so ... well, E.V.I.L., that I think your superbrain is about to be defeated. And let's face it: I'm (almost) never wrong!

All right, it's time to find out if you truly are a genius.
Here's your last puzzle.

(If you need a hint, see the bottom of the page.)

●●●●●●●●●●●●●●●●●●●●●●●●●●●●●●●●●●●●●●

————— ————— ————— ————— ————— —————   ————— ————— —————
Ch 8, Q2 Ch 6, Q3 Ch 2, Q3 Ch 9, Q3 Ch 3, Q1 Ch 4, Q3   Ch 5, Q1 Ch 9, Q2 Ch 3, Q4

        ————— ————— —————   ————— ————— —————
        Ch 2, Q1 Ch 8, Q1 Ch 5, Q3   Ch 3, Q3 Ch 6, Q4 Ch 4, Q4

                ————— ————— ————— ————— —————
                Ch 5, Q4 Ch 4, Q2 Ch 2, Q2 Ch 9, Q1 Ch 5, Q2

        ————— ————— ————— ————— ————— ————— —————
        Ch 4, Q1 Ch 6, Q2 Ch 7, Q3 Ch 7, Q4 Ch 3, Q2 Ch 6, Q1 Ch 8, Q3

                ————— ————— ————— ————— ————— .
                Ch 8, Q4 Ch 7, Q2 Ch 7, Q1 Ch 2, Q4 Ch 9, Q4

Puzzle Trivia:
Did you know
that A=1, Z=26
is a basic
Letter-Number
cypher?

ONLY A TRUE GENIUS COULD HAVE
SOLVED THIS PUZZLE! NOT EVEN
ALBERT EINSTEIN OR ISAAC NEWTON
COULD SOLVE IT, BUT I DARE YOU . . . TRY
TO PROVE ME WRONG. YOU MAY HAVE
OUTSMARTED ME ONCE OR TWICE
BEFORE, BUT THIS TIME I WILL NOT BE
DEFEATED!

HINT: Use your recorded answers from the end-of-chapter quizzes.

Nooooo! You've outsmarted me again!

I had your brain in my vicious grasp and you managed to slip away. I've got to hand it to you, Mastermind—that was one brilliant victory.

But did you really think I would let you go just like that? Ha! I won't admit defeat. I've put out a notice to my cronies at E.V.I.L. offering a reward for your capture. Now every brainy baddie on Earth will be looking for you—MUAHAHA! You'll be in my cranial custody before you can blink. You might as well give up now, Mastermind, because your noggin is a goner!

I vow this with all of my horrible heart: When I catch you, your brain will be mine, once and for all!

Until next time,

Ima Genius

Ima Genius
E.V.I.L. Mastermind

WANTED: MASTERMIND

DANGEROUS BRAIN ON THE LOOSE. APPROACH WITH CAUTION!

KNOWN ALIASES:
Mental Merlin, Einstein 2.0, The Nogginator

ATTENTION, EVIL GENIUSES OF EARTH: A Mastermind has recently escaped our clutches and is now at large. This brain is armed—with knowledge!—and dangerous. Instead of joining forces with us, this maniac brainiac is intent on using that prodigious mental power for the benefit of those goons over at G.O.O.D. This puts our standing as the superior society of smarts at risk!

If you have any information on the whereabouts of this intellectual offender, please contact Ima Genius immediately. With the power of our collective craniums, this Mastermind will be back under our control in no time—and then, we'll use that brainpower to take over the world!

REWARD:

For information leading to the apprehension of this heinous Mastermind, you will receive four (4) tickets for you and your family to E.V.I.L. Land Water Park.

QUIZ AND PUZZLE **ANSWERS**

CHAPTER 1

Puzzle A, p. 10

There are many possible solutions. We've shown you only three below: a.) fish b.) 2 arrows c.) tree

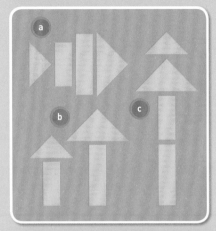

Puzzle B, p. 11

Each object's name and color start with the same letter. Therefore, the bear should be black or brown, and the rose should be red.

Puzzle C, p. 11

Puzzle D, p. 11

Changing the R into C in each word will change the entire list!
ROT .... COT
BARK .... BACK
ROAST .... COAST

CHAPTER 2

Brain Puzzle, p. 19

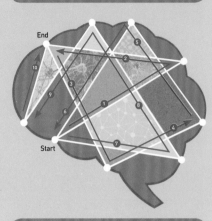

Letter Swap, p. 22

Scorpions glow under ultraviolet light, but scientists do not know why. (Letters N & T were swapped!)

Rebus, p. 23

"Somewhere Over the Rainbow" (The word "SOMEWHERE" appears OVER the RAINBOW.)

Spectrumtacular!, p. 30

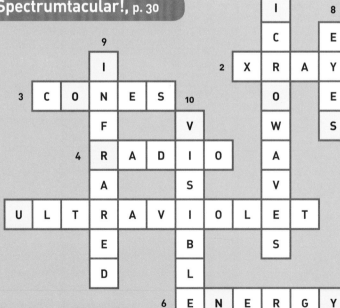

Bonus answer: YOUR VISION

Cat Eyes, p. 26

Who can see better, you humans with more cones to see far-off details, including small stones,

Or a cat like me who has rods for night vision to hunt my prey, with deadly precision.

While your eyes mix greens, reds, and blues, I see very few colors, in limited hues.

You humans see great during the day, when cats lounge, sleep, and play.

While we lack your power to see so far, consider this, my super star....

As I scrunch down low, weaving through the grasses, can you imagine me, a cat, wearing your glasses?

Butterfly Code, p. 27

Red Butterfly: "COME FLY WITH ME"
Blue Butterfly: "THIS IS MY FLOWER"

Triangulation, p. 29

Move any of the orange triangles into the center of the largest yellow triangle to split it into three, leaving you with a total of five complete yellow triangles.

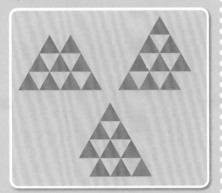

Color Confusion, p. 31

The eyes and mouths on both faces are the same color (blue)! Their different backgrounds make them look like two different colors. Don't believe it? Check it out:

Riding the Radio Waves, p. 31

We use radio waves to talk to astronauts in space.

Hidden Objects, p. 32

We see these images, but that doesn't mean you don't see more!
a. 6 arrows
b. 2 diamonds
c. 3 X's
d. 4 houses: 2 right side up, 2 upside down (only one outlined in image)

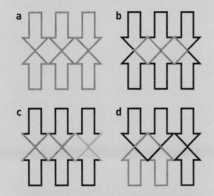

Decoding RGB, p. 33

Quiz, pp. 34–35

RECORD YOUR ANSWERS HERE

1	2	3	4
18	5	13	15

CHAPTER 3

Connection, p. 43

Start by placing the word "CONNECTION" in the yellow squares. From there, you can fill in the rest of the words.

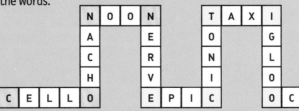

Brain Puzzle, p. 37

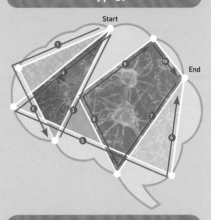

Letter Swap, p. 40

The longest human tongue in the world is almost four inches from the tip to the top lip. (Letters I & N were swapped!)

Rebus, p. 41

"Everything is Upside Down" (The word "EVERYTHING" is literally upside down.)

Line 'Em Up, p. 44

The black lines are the exact same length. Your mind uses the background of an object to judge its size. The yellow pole makes it look like the top line is in the distance, so your brain decides it must be longer.

Brain at Work, p. 45

Pain signals travel to your brain very slowly—at just two feet per second. That's why if you stub your toe, two or three seconds pass before you feel the pain.

Ambigram, p. 45

MASTERMIND

Mega Mix-Up, p. 48

The last square is the only one that has the correct label for the picture.

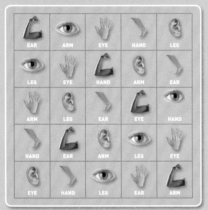

Circulation, p. 49

There are 60,000 miles of blood vessels in your body—enough to wrap around the Earth two and a half times.

Decoding the Human Body, p. 50

There are 100 million neurons in your gut.

Toy Thief, p. 51

Alexa held the note up to the mirror to discover the location, date, and time of when the thief was meeting the buyer. The buyer had written the information backward!

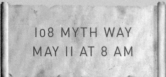

I08 MYTH WAY
MAY II AT 8 AM

Quiz, pp. 52–53

RECORD YOUR ANSWERS HERE

❶	❷	❸	❹
22	5	1	12

CHAPTER 4

Brain Puzzle, p. 55

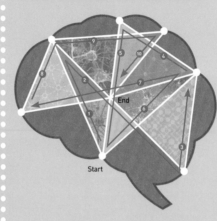

Letter Swap, p. 58

Titanoboa lived 60 million years ago. It was fifty feet long, the longest snake ever! (Letters E & L were swapped!)

Rebus, p. 59

"Mirror, Mirror on the Wall." (This expression was made famous by the Wicked Queen in the story of *Snow White*.)

Wordless Search, p. 62

We found 14 words from this chapter in this wordless search. Of course, you may have found more words, which means you're extra bright!
Word list: Brain, Clue, Conscious, Control, Eyes, Genius, Mind, Nose, Predict, Sense, Sounds, Test, Thalamus, Think

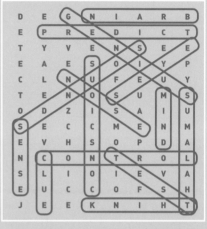

Cryptogram, p. 63

MRI machines use magnets to take pictures of your insides.

Count on It, p. 65

See those numbers to the left of the puzzle text? They indicate which word in that sentence is part of a secret message.

The secret message is: "Your name may determine your job."

6	It is time to test your brain by giving you a puzzle without instructions.
6	Have you looked at its name yet?
2	It may help you figure out how to solve it.
3	If you determine the secret I'm hiding, *count* yourself lucky.
5	By all means, use your unconscious mind.
11	Just don't expect me to help you; that's not my job!

—Ima Genius (but are you?)

Spotty Business, p. 67

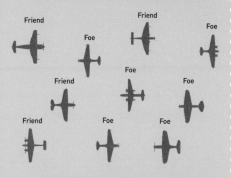

Friend · Friend · Foe · Foe · Friend · Foe · Foe · Friend · Foe · Foe

M. Emery's Mix-Up, p. 68

The only information that you would not figure out from the five facts provided is which city Justin Time and Annie Moment are from. The hint for this piece of information is in the directions, where you're reminded that a person's name may be associated to certain qualities about him/her ... such as the name of his/her city. Annie Moment comes from Ann Arbor, MI, and Justin Time comes from Jasper, TN.

STUDENT	Justin Time
CITY	Jasper, TN
AGE	17

STUDENT	Annie Moment
CITY	Ann Arbor, MI
AGE	18

STUDENT	Dennis Tree
CITY	Dallas, TX
AGE	20

STUDENT	Ken D'Corn
CITY	Clinton, CT
AGE	21

No Manners, p. 69

Butterflies taste with their feet.

Riddles, p. 69

1. Table
2. Turn the hourglass on its side.
3. The letter *D*

Quiz, pp. 70–71

RECORD YOUR ANSWERS HERE

1	2	3	4
12	18	5	4

CHAPTER 5

Brain Puzzle, p. 73

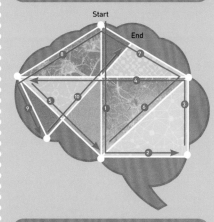

What's Your Number?, p. 75

I found your keys. You left them in the piano.

Letter Swap, p. 76

Not getting enough sleep can make you remember things that did not actually happen. (Letters T & E were swapped!)

Rebus, p. 77

"Fading Away"
(The word "AWAY" is fading.)

Find That Memory, p. 81

Closing your eyes can help you remember.

Total Recall, p. 84

H I P P O ✚ C A M P ✚ U S

S H O R T ▢ T E R M

E A R L Y

BONUS: M E M O R Y

A Place for Everything, p. 85

T	H	A	N	K	S
F	O	R		T	H	E
M	E	M	O	R	I	E	S

Word Switch, p. 86

Giraffe = Fence
Flower = Ball
Hamburger = Bike
Lion = Kite
Worms = Water

A dog named Jack loved to play outside with a ball. His buddy Terri tossed his ball too far and it soared over the fence. When Jack went around the fence, he couldn't find the ball, but he spotted a kite flying through the air. A boy was zipping down the street on his bike while holding onto the string of the kite. Jack chased the bike and the kite. The boy on the bike suddenly stopped. The kite floated down and landed on the fence. And right below it, Jack spotted another ball. He scooped up the ball, slipped through the hole in the fence, and headed home. Jack had enjoyed chasing the ball, bike, and kite, but he had a nice cold bowl of water waiting for him at home.

Shape That Memory, p. 87

There are eight occurrences.

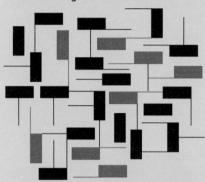

Quiz, pp. 88–89

RECORD YOUR ANSWERS HERE

1	2	3	4
1	14	4	7

CHAPTER 6

Brain Puzzle, p. 91

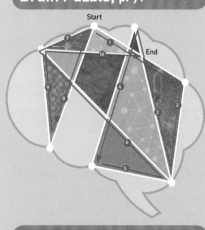

Start
End

Letter Swap, p. 94

On average, a person makes 396 friends in a lifetime. Six of those will be best friends. (Letters A & F were swapped!)

Rebus, p. 95

"Genius" (The image of the genie + the word "Yes" = "Genius.")

Healthy Living, p. 98

Having a **strong network** of **friends** could help you live longer.

Missing Friend, p. 98

To the right of every right-facing white dolphin is a left-facing blue horse.

Friendship Points, p. 99

Here are some of the 90 possible words:

5-LETTER WORDS

1. DINER   6. FRIED   11. SHINE
2. FIEND   7. HIRED   12. SHRED
3. FINED   8. PRIDE   13. SIREN
4. FIRED   9. RINSE   14. SPEND
5. FRESH   10. RIPEN   15. SPINE

6-LETTER WORDS

1. FINISH   6. PERISH   11. SHINER
2. FISHED   7. REFIND   12. SHRINE
3. FRIEND   8. RESHIP   13. SNIPER
4. HINDER   9. RINSED   14. SPIDER
5. INSIDE   10. SHINED 15. SPINED

7-LETTER WORDS

1. DISHIER 5. NERDISH 9. SHRINED
2. FISHIER 6. PINFISH 10. SPINIER
3. INSIDER 7. REDFISH
4. INSPIRE 8. SHINIER

8-LETTER WORDS

1. FIENDISH   4. INSPIRED
2. FINISHED   5. REFINISH
3. FINISHER

Two of a Kind, p. 101

We are wearing the same genes!

Mastermind Network, p. 102

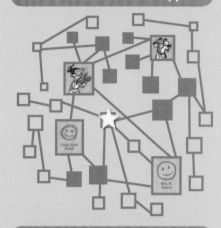

Amazing Choice, p. 103

Genius Advice, p. 104

Think for yourself.

Nonconformist, p. 105

Quiz, pp. 106–107

CHAPTER 7

Brain Puzzle, p. 109

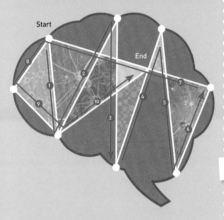

Start

End

Translation Time, p. 111

Hickory, dickory, dock.
The mouse ran up the clock.
The clock struck one,
The mouse ran down,
Hickory dickory dock.

"Hickory Dickory Dock." While most of the words were made up, you could have figured out the name of the rhyme by a few key words, the rhythm, and the "feel" of the poem.

Letter Swap, p. 112

The official language of Cambodia, Khmer, has the longest alphabet—74 letters. (Letters A & T were swapped!)

Rebus, p. 113

"Straight Down the Middle"
(The word "STRAIGHT" is going DOWN the word "MIDDLE.")

Sounds Like a Winner, p. 116

WORDS that have the same **PRONUNCIATION** but different **MEANINGS** are **HOMONYMS.**

Sign of the Times, p. 117

Thomas Hopkins Gallaudet

Ironic Fear, p. 120

All of the clues fit together to form one single but veeerrryyyy long word:

HIPPOPOTOMONSTROSEQUIPPEDALIOPHOBIA.

This is the fear of long words, which is why we wouldn't expect anyone who has this fear to be able to say or write the name of his/her fear!

Pesky Palindromes, p. 120

L EVE L   K AYA K
R ADA R   H ANNA H
R OTO R   R ACECA R
S OLO S

Auto Incorrect, p. 121

I was searching for recipes online, hoping to make some tasty sandwiches. Can you make some coleslaw? We need enough for forty people. You should also bring that coffee ice cream from your freezer. This is going to be an awesome picnic! I might even try jumping rope with the kids this year!

Love,
Your Auntie Rebel

Flick of the Wrist, p. 121

There was more than one answer for many of these. Did you come up with these words or with your own, Mastermind?

BLACK - L = BACK
NEAT - A = NET
WINDOW - N = WIDOW
GOAT - G = OAT
POUT - U = POT
PAIN - A = PIN
GRAVE - G = RAVE
DIME - E = DIM

Will It Fit?, p. 122

BANGKOK, THAILAND: Wait, didn't we say this was one of the longest place names in the world? As you can see, Bangkok, Thailand, is a short name! That's because "Bangkok" is the name foreigners call the city. To Thais, the city's full name is Krung Thep Mahanakhon Amon Rattanako-sin Mahinthara Ayuthaya Mahadilok Phop Noppharat Ratchathani Burirom Udomratchaniwet Mahasathan Amon Piman Awatan Sathit Sakkathattiya Witsanukam Prasit. Now that's long!

Road Trip, p. 122

1. SEATTLE
2. BALTIMORE
3. COLUMBUS
4. MILWAUKEE
5. HOUSTON
6. KANSAS CITY
7. NEW ORLEANS
8. MINNEAPOLIS
9. ANNAPOLIS
10. BISMARCK
11. SACRAMENTO

No Rhyme This Time, p. 123

1. BULB
2. ORANGE
3. ANGEL
4. SILVER
5. MONTH
6. FALSE
7. WALRUS
8. WASP

Quiz, pp. 124–125

CHAPTER 8

Brain Puzzle, p. 127

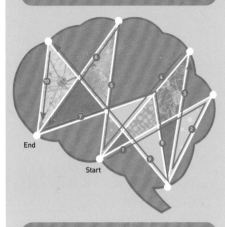

Letter Swap, p. 130

Sea otters hold hands when they sleep to prevent drifting away from one another. (Letters O & H were swapped!)

Rebus, p. 131

"Shattered Dreams" or "Broken Dreams" (The word "DREAMS" has been shattered, or broken.)

Jokes, p. 134

1. Log some *z's*
2. At *sss*-lumber parties

Catch Some Z's, p. 134

If you only count the uniform Z's like this one Z, there are 37 in this puzzle: 20 small + 12 medium + 5 large.

If you include the Z's that have different length tops and bottoms like these Z Z, there are many more than 37!

Doggie Dreams, p. 135

Items in top picture, changed in bottom:
1. Red toe and heel on sock
2. Line on meat
3. Cherry on ice cream
4. Dog bowl color
5. Flower to right of doghouse
6. Blue doughnut design
7. Letter S from "Sandy"
8. Paw print on ball
9. Spot on dog's back
10. Ball in grass
11. Uppermost dream bubble
12. Stick in grass
13. Dog bone in grass

Count to 12, p. 137

If you put the puzzle pieces together, then it becomes clear that the missing numbers are 3 (green square), 9 (red square), and 12 (blue square).

1	2	3	4
5	6	7	8
9	10	11	12

Color That Dream, p. 138

Before color television was invented, only 15% of people dreamed in color. Now 75% dream in color.

Sleeping Animals, p. 139

The red letters in the names of the other animals spell out the answer: GIRAFFE.

Bedtime Wish, p. 140

SLEEP TIGHT

Dreams, p. 140

1. Unscramble all the letters to get the solution: DAYDREAM.
2. Knight+Mare (a female horse) = NIGHTMARE
3. S+WE+E+T + Dreams = SWEET DREAMS

The Framework of Sleep, p. 141

Quiz, pp. 142–143

	1	2	3	4
RECORD YOUR ANSWERS HERE	5	18	19	2

CHAPTER 9

Brain Puzzle, p. 145

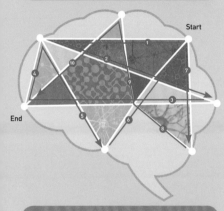

Letter Swap, p. 148

Patients can be awake during brain surgery because there are no pain receptors in the brain. (Letters I & R were swapped!)

Rebus, p. 149

"Thundercloud" (Sound out the letters "TH" and then say where they are … UNDER the CLOUD.)

Deal of the Day, p. 152

Bat and Ball: B (The price is $2 cheaper when you pay the entire amount up front.)
Robot: B (Robot A appears cheaper, but once you add the shipping cost, you see the total cost is 4¢ more.)
Cookie: A ($3.60 per dozen is cheaper. It is the same as 30¢ per cookie!)

Lunch, p. 157

Brain tissue has a texture that is very similar to tofu.

It Boggles The Mind, p. 155

While you will find many words in this puzzle, the following 11 are found in this chapter:
1. ALGAE
2. ANT(S)
3. BRAIN(S)
4. CONTROL
5. LAB
6. MENTAL
7. MOUSE
8. NEURON
9. SCIENTIST
10. SMART
11. TEST

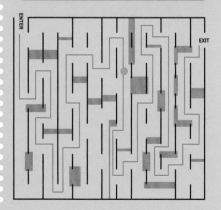

Sneaky Advertising, p. 156

These words appear in the text: mouse, mice, rat, roach, moth, bear.

Larry's Limousine Service—The limo used by cheese lovers.
Salami Central is rodent free.
Pandora Taxi Company—We're known for our cleanliness.
Marve's Motel—Where a superhero achieves fame!
Wayne's Wrestling Ring—Hear the roar of sumo thunder.
Crazy Costumes—Wardrobe area is danger free.

Zombie Zigzag, p. 153

ENTER
EXIT

Confusing Squares, p. 157

First, cross out the color-shape combinations that have an exact match.

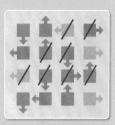

Next, match the remaining shapes to the empty ones in the bottom row so you know which colors to use where.

Buried in the Past, p. 158

HEART LUNGS INTESTINES STOMACH LIVER BRAIN

Unauthorized Experiment, p. 159

Olivia and Daniel are the culprits.

Quiz, pp. 160–161

	1	2	3	4
RECORD YOUR ANSWERS HERE	5	12	15	23

Final Exam, p. 163

"REMOVE ALL RED AND GREEN LETTERS BELOW."

Once you follow these instructions, Masterminds, you'll reveal the hidden message: "YOU ARE A TRUE MASTERMIND!"

Index

Illustration Credits

SS=Shutterstock, DT=Dreamstime, GI=Getty Images

Illustrations of Ima Genius and Atom by Kevin Rechin

Cover, (CTR LE), R. Gino Santa Maria/SS; Cover, (LO RT), Javier Brosch/SS; Cover (LO LE), HomeStudio/SS; Cover (UP LE), DNY59/GT; Cover (UP RT), Africa Studio/SS;

Front matter: 3 (LO LE), R. Gino Santa Maria/SS; 3 (LO LE), Ckarzx/DT; 3 (LO RT), HomeStudio/SS; 3 (UP), DNY59/GT; 4 (LO), HomeStudio/SS; 4 (UP), Africa Studio/SS;5 (LO), Javier Brosch/SS; 5 (UP), Africa Studio/SS;

Chapter 1: 6 (UP), donatas1205/SS; 7, azerberber/GT; 8 (LO RT), Vitaly Korovin; 10, adventtr/GT; 11 (UP CTR LE), photographyfirm/SS; 11 (UP CTR RT), Monika Adamczyk/DT; 11 (UP LE), annt/SS; 11 (UP RT), Ivanbogun/DT; 12-13 (UP), Matjaz Preseren/SS; 12 (LO LE), Africa Studio/SS; 12 (LO RT), R. Gino Santa Maria/SS; 12 (CTR LE), pictore/GT; 12 (CTR RT), GeorgiosArt/GT; 13 (LO LE), Alhovik/SS; 13 (LO RT), slpix/SS;13 (CTR LE), Ken Brown/GT; 13 (CTR RT), stocksnapper/GT; 14 (UP), David Crockett/GT; 15, vasabii/SS; 16 (LO), Viktarm/DT; 16 (UP), Sebastian Kaulitzki/SS; 17 (LO), Jaroslav Moravcik/SS; 17 (UP), Sergey Nivens/SS;

Chapter 2: 18 (UP), Fly_dragonfly/SS; 19 (LO), Andrea Danti/SS; 20 (LO), Richard Valdez/DT; 20 (UP), thailoei92/SS; 21 (CTR), Photographerv8/DT; 21 (LO), Patrick Foto/SS; 21 (UP), Johnbell/DT; 22 (UP), Garsya/SS; 23 (UP), Jesús Eloy Ramos Lara/DT; 23 (LO RT), Tharakorn Arunothai/SS; 24 (LO), Kirsanov Valeriy Vladimirovich/SS; 24 (UP), Oksana Kuzmina/SS; 25 (LO), Vitaly Titov/SS; 25 (UP), Giulio_Fornasar/SS; 26, Smiltena/SS; 27, suns07butterfly/SS; 28, Concetta Antico; 28 (UP), PeterPhoto123/SS; 29, John Anderson/DT; 30 (LO), suns07butterfly/SS; 30 (UP), Milous Chab/DT; 33, ifong/SS;34 (UP LE), Mega Pixel/SS; 34 (UP RT), Tatiana Popova/SS; 34 (LO), Federico Rostagno/SS; 35 (CTR LE), Alena Ozerova/DT; 35 (UP), Ameng Wu/GT;

Chapter 3: 36 (UP), Duplass/SS; 37 (LO), Rawpixel/SS; 38, Simon Ritter/Alamy Stock Photo; 38 (UP), Oksana Mizina/SS; 39 (CTR), Matthew Rakola/NGP; 39 (LO), Matthew Rakola/NGP; 39 (UP), Tiplyashina Evgeniya/SS; 42 (LO), Valentina Razumova/SS; 42 (UP), Paul Avis/Alamy Stock Photo; 43 (UP), Media for Medical/GT; 44, R-O-M-A/SS; 45, Mohol/DT; 46, John Storey/GT; 47 (LO), Glen Chapman/GT; 47 (UP), Photos 12/Alamy Stock Photo; 47 (UP RT), irin-k/SS; 48 (Arm), Ron Chapple/DT; 48 (Ear), Ninell/DT; 48 (Eye), Anton Samsonov/DT; 48 (Hand), Antonio Guillem/SS; 49, Fisherss/SS; 50, villorejo/SS; 52 (LO), Chunumunu/SS; 53 (CTR), Susan Schmitz/SS; 53 (UP), belushi/SS;

Chapter 4: 54, annt/SS; 55, D_Gosha/SS; 56 (LO LE), Ervin Monn/SS; 56 (UP), DenisFilm/SS; 57, Eric Isselée/SS; 57 (LO), Scott Camazine/GT; 57 (LO RT), Stefan Hermans/DT; 59 (LO), arogant/SS; 59 (UP), Room27/SS; 60 (LO), Steve Gettle/Minden Pictures; 60 (UP), Jodi Jacobson/GT; 61 (LO), Eric Isselée/SS; 61 (UP), Eric Isselée/GT; 62, Budda/DT; 64 (LO), espies/SS; 64 (UP), Glenn Frank/GT; 65 (UP), JonoUK/GT; 67, Dwight Smith/SS; 68, Dimedrol68/SS; 69, Irochka/DT; 70 (LO), E+/GT; 71, Fly_dragonfly/SS; 71 (CTR), Alan Murphy/BIA/Minden Pictures;

Chapter 5: 72, M. Dykstra/SS; 73, Nikolya/SS; 74 (LO), Flashon Studio/SS; 74 (UP), nyvltart/GT; 75, Leo Blanchette/SS; 75 (LO), Steven Russell Smith Photos/SS; 78 (LO), Eric Isselée/SS; 78 (UP), Talvi/SS; 79 (LE), zhengzaishuru/SS; 79 (LO), Joseph Gareri/GT; 79 (UP), QiuJu Song/SS; 81, Bohbeh/SS; 82, Nicku/DT; 83, pukach/SS; 83 (LE), Maks Narodenko/SS; 83 (UP RT), IrinaK/SS; 85, E+/GT; 86 (LE), Alex Hubenov/SS; 86 (RT), Gena73/SS; 88 (LO), IrinaK/SS; 89 (UP), Sallyeva/DT;

Chapter 6: 90, Ermolaev Alexander/SS; 91, holbox/SS; 92 (LO), Gino Santa Maria/SS; 92 (UP), tratong/SS; 93 (LO), Javier Brosch/SS; 93 (LO LE), zhaoyan/SS; 93 (UP), Hero Images/GT; 95 (UP), Anneka/SS; 96, Isselée/DT; 97 (LO), Taiga/SS; 97 (UP LE), nikonphotog/GT; 97 (UP RT), Willyam Bradberry/SS; 100, Scott Richardson/SS; 101, Torsakarin/DT; 104, Nemanja Tomic/DT; 106 (LO), Aaron Amat/SS; 107 (UP), Elena Larina/SS;

Chapter 7: 108 (RT), photosync/SS; 109, Syda Productions/SS; 110 (LO), Ostancov Vladislav/DT; 110 (UP), Africa Studio/SS; 111, Ryan Carter/SS; 114 (LE), Eric Isselée/SS; 114 (RT), Cathleen A Clapper/SS; 115 (LO), Kerstin Meyer/GT; 115 (UP), Brian Skerry/National Geographic Creative; 117, robynleigh/SS; 118 (LO), Joseph Calev/SS; 119 (LO LE), Vitaly Korovin/SS; 119 (CTR LE), glenda/SS; 119 (CTR RT), Gergo Kazsimer/DT; 119 (LE), successo images/SS; 119 (RT), Javier Brosch/SS; 119 (UP), AlenKadr/SS; 120 (Bee), Isselée/DT; 120 (Bike), Vladyslav Starozhylov/SS; 120 (Hippo), Gubin Yury/SS; 120 (Monster), Albert Ziganshin/SS; 120 (Pot), Clearvista/DT; 120 (Rose), oksana2010/SS; 122 (RT), Nomad_Soul/SS; 124 (LO), Lucie Lang/SS; 125, Andrea Izzotti/SS;

Chapter 8: 126, Pavel Bobrovskiy/SS; 127, poutnik/SS; 128-129, sasimoto/SS; 128 (UP), Picsfive/SS; 132, abezikus/GT; 133 (CTR), Gudkov Andrey/SS; 133 (LO), Matthew Maran/NPL/Minden Pictures; 133 (UP), Jurgen and Christine Sohns/FLPA/Minden Pictures; 134, GraphicsRF/SS; 135 (Baseball), Matt Benoit/SS; 135 (Bone), photoDISC/NGS; 135 (Cat), Ruslan Semichev/SS; 135 (Dog), Artsilense/SS; 135 (Dog food), Africa Studio/SS; 135 (Doghouse), E+/GT; 135 (Flowers), AlenKadr/SS; 135 (Grass), robert_s/SS; 135 (Ice cream), Dan Kosmayer/SS; 135 (Pizza), bestv/SS; 135 (Ring), hd connelly/SS; 135 (Sock), alexandre zveiger/SS; 135 (Steak), Pavlo_K/SS; 135 (Stick), Danny Smythe/DT; 135 (Tennis ball), Richard Peterson/SS; 136 (LO LE), Kuttelvaserova Stuchelova/SS; 136 (LO RT), Bettmann/GT; 136 (UP), Bettmann/GT; 137 (UP), Vlue/SS; 138, Rose Carson/SS; 139 (Cat), Nichacha/DT; 139 (Dog), ArtSilense/SS; 139 (Ferret), Kuricheva Ekaterina/SS; 139 (Fish), Andrew Ilyasov/E+/GI; 139 (Mouse), Roger Tidman/FLPA/Minden Pictures; 139 (Squirrel), Gerald Marella/SS; 139 (Tiger), Coffeemill/SS; 140 (LO LE), Nejron Photo/SS; 140 (LO RT), Eric Isselée/SS; 140 (UP), Ted Russell/GT; 142 (LO), Smit/SS; 143 (UP), Katherine McGovern/SS;

Chapter 9: 144 (UP), Suzanne Tucker/SS; 145, David Crockett/SS; 146 (Bulb), Chones/SS; 146 (Mouse), Kuttelvaserova Stuchelova/SS; 147 (LO), Fotos593/SS; 147 (UP), Getmilitaryphotos/SS; 149 (UP), Halil I. Inci/DT; 150, Jagodka/SS; 151 (LO LE), Thailand Wildlife/Alamy Stock Photo; 151 (LO RT), Anand Varma/National Geographic Creative; 151 (UP), Papik/SS; 152 (LO), Homydesign/DT; 152 (LO LE), Mega Pixel/SS; 152 (CTR), Davinci/DT; 152 (UP), Buriy/DT; 154 (LE), John B. Carnett/GT; 154 (LO), Sciepro/GT; 155, Henning Dalhoff/Science Source; 156 (CTR LE), Igorr/DT; 156 (CTR RT), Ken Backer/DT; 156 (LO LE), altrendo images/GT; 156 (LO RT), Andrew B Hall/SS; 156 (UP LE), Kamski59/DT; 156 (UP RT), Yuriy Chaban/DT; 157 (LO), Charles Brutlag/DT; 157 (UP), Gmeviphoto/SS; 158 (CTR), DEA Picture Library/GT; 158 (LE), Universal Images Group/GT; 158 (LO RT), Oliver Hoffmann/SS; 159 (UP), Echo/GT; 160 (LO), photolinc/SS; 161 (CTR), irin-k/SS; 161 (UP), pio3/SS; 165, Taddeus/SS

For Dave, the best brainiac there is. —SWD

Since 1888, the National Geographic Society has funded more than 12,000 research, exploration, and preservation projects around the world. The Society receives funds from National Geographic Partners, LLC, funded in part by your purchase. A portion of the proceeds from this book supports this vital work. To learn more, visit natgeo.com/info.

NATIONAL GEOGRAPHIC and Yellow Border Design are trademarks of the National Geographic Society, used under license.

For more information, visit nationalgeographic.com, call 1-800-647-5463, or write to the following address:

National Geographic Partners
1145 17th Street N.W.
Washington, D.C. 20036-4688 U.S.A.

Visit us online at nationalgeographic.com/books

For librarians and teachers: ngchildrensbooks.org

More for kids from National Geographic:
kids.nationalgeographic.com

For information about special discounts for bulk purchases, please contact National Geographic Books Special Sales: specialsales@natgeo.com

For rights or permissions inquiries, please contact National Geographic Books Subsidiary Rights: bookrights@natgeo.com

Art directed by Amanda Larsen
Designed by Greg Jackson/Thinkpen Design

Trade paperback ISBN: 978-1-4263-2423-9

Printed in China
17/RRDS/1

NATIONAL GEOGRAPHIC KiDS
5,000 AWESOME FACTS 3
(About Everything!)

Wonder how many AWESOME FACTS your BRAIN can RETAIN?

Did you know that our planet Earth is about 4.55 billion years old? That a pizza was delivered to the International Space Station? Or that "sedatephobia" is an intense fear of silence? Here are some more wild and wacky facts that will make your head spin!

15 FERRIS WHEEL FACTS TO MAKE YOUR HEAD SPIN

1 The **WORLD'S FIRST** Ferris wheel—designed by engineer George Ferris for the Chicago World's Fair in 1893—cost 50 cents to ride and could hold **MORE THAN 2,000 RIDERS** at once.

2 Original Ferris wheels were turned by powerful **STEAM ENGINES.** Most modern wheels run on **ELECTRICITY.**

3 You can ride a **HUMAN-POWERED** Ferris wheel in India, with park employees using their **BODY WEIGHT** to help turn the wheel.

4 The **NEW YORK WHEEL** will tower more than **60 STORIES** over **NEW YORK CITY,** making it one of the **WORLD'S TALLEST** Ferris wheels.

5 A roller coaster whips through the middle of the **BIG O** wheel in Tokyo, Japan—one of the only Ferris wheels to operate without a **CENTER AXLE** or **SPOKES.**

6 The **PACIFIC WHEEL** in Santa Monica, California, U.S.A., is the only entirely **SOLAR-POWERED** Ferris wheel on the **PLANET.**

7 The **CAPTAIN WHEEL** outside of Washington, D.C., U.S.A., is decorated with 1.6 million **LED** lights that **CHANGE COLOR** to the beat of **MUSIC.**

8 Turkmenistan is home to the **LARGEST ENCLOSED** Ferris wheel in the world, a 156-foot (47.5-m)-tall ride built inside a **GLASS** and **MARBLE** structure.

6:30

9 Despite being damaged during WORLD WAR II, the 120-year-old Wiener Riesenrad in VIENNA, AUSTRIA, still spins with 15 of its original 30 cars.

10 The TRANSPORTABLE Roue de Paris wheel—that has popped up in PARIS, ENGLAND, BANGKOK, and AMSTERDAM—can be **DISMANTLED** in 60 HOURS and built in 72 HOURS.

11 Each year, more than **3.7 MILLION PEOPLE** take a spin on the LONDON EYE, Europe's largest Ferris wheel built to mark the **NEW MILLENNIUM** in 2000.

12 It takes **30 MINUTES** to make a **FULL ROTATION** on the **SINGAPORE FLYER,** a massive wheel that's nearly as tall as the **WASHINGTON MONUMENT.**

13 An artist created a **PEDAL-POWERED** Ferris wheel, powered by a TRIO OF RIDERS simultaneously pedaling to propel and rotate the ride.

14 The TIANJIN EYE looms large over a SIX-LANE BRIDGE in northern China, with cars and pedestrians **PASSING BELOW** the 394-FOOT (120-M) wheel.

15 With a **TIME DISPLAY** at the center of a giant Ferris wheel, the COSMO CLOCK 21 in Yokohama, Japan, can claim to be the world's LARGEST CLOCK.

8 5,000 AWESOME FACTS 3

※ YOU HAVE LEARNED **16** FACTS

5,000 AWESOME FACTS 3 **9**

NATIONAL GEOGRAPHIC KiDS

Ima Genius here, your host for *Brain Bogglers*. Once upon a time I was a budding brain builder intent on turning puny pinheads into smarty-pants worthy of my time and energy. But these days I find myself at odds with my fellow master-minds, you rivals of my reasoning. I think it's time to duke it out in a cranium-to-cranium challenge!

In *Brain Bogglers* you'll go head-to-head against super-evil scholar Ima Genius with tons of brain-building puzzles, tests, and tricky teasers. Explore the mysteries of your mind, learn about all the incredible ways your thinker ticks, and flex those mental muscles! With Ima and her genius dog, Atom, as your hosts, it's a funny and fun, silly and smart way to build your budding brain!

Jam-packed with puzzles, this book features:

- curious codes
- mind-bending mazes
- optical illusions
- tricky wordplay
- hidden pictures
- crosswords and word searches
- fill-in-the-blanks
- brain teasers
- crowd pleasers

And so much more!

CHECK OUT OUR OTHER BRAIN-BOGGLING ACTIVITY BOOK!

kids.nationalgeographic.com

$12.99 U.S. / $16.99 CAN / £8.99 UK
ISBN 978-1-4263-2423-9 / PRINTED IN CHINA

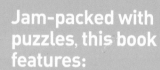